TRUE

THE NATION

PAUL BERNARDO and KARLA HOMOLKA
"The Ken and Barbie Killers"

Volume 3

by Peter Vronsky

Crimes Canada
True Crimes That Shocked The Nation

ISBN-13: 978-1987902037
ISBN-10: 1987902033

Published by:

VP Publication an Imprint of
RJ Parker Publishing, Inc.

Crimes Canada: True Crimes That Shocked the Nation

Series Introduction

In this multi-volume series edited by crime historian Dr. Peter Vronsky and true crime author and publisher RJ Parker, some of Canada's most notorious shocking crimes will be described and explored, including some of the cases mentioned above.

Crimes Canada: True Crimes that Shocked the Nation, will feature a series of Canadian true crime books published by VP Publication (Vronsky & Parker), an imprint of RJ Parker Publishing, Inc., one of the world's leading Indie publishers of true crime.

Peter Vronsky is the bestselling author of Serial Killers: The Method and Madness of Monsters and Female Serial Killers: How and Why Women Become Monsters while RJ Parker is not only a successful Indie publisher but also the author of books like, Serial Killers Abridged: An Encyclopedia of 100 Serial Killers, Social Media Monsters: Internet Killers, Parents Who Killed Their Children: Filicide, and Serial Killer Groupies. Both are Canadians and have teamed up to share shocking Canadian true crime cases not only with fellow Canadian readers but with Americans and world readers as well, who

will be shocked and horrified by just how evil and sick "nice" Canadians can be when they go bad.

Finally, the editors invite their established Canadian fellow authors and aspiring authors to submit proposals or manuscripts to VP Publication at CrimesCanada@RJParkerPublishing.com.

VP Publication is a new frontier Indie publisher, offering their published authors a generous royalty agreement payable within three months of publishing and aggressive online marketing support. Unlike many so-called "publishers" that are nothing but vanity presses in disguise, VP Publication does not charge authors in advance for submitting their proposal or manuscripts, nor do we charge authors if we choose to publish their works. We pay you, and pay well.

Background

In Ontario, Canada, in 1991-1992 two teenage high school girls vanished near their homes or schools in normally safe and cozy small-town communities. One girl was found dismembered and encased in ready-mix cement blocks dumped in the shallows of a fishing pond while the other was found naked in a roadside ditch, her body washed and hair cut off in what police suspected was some kind of bizarre trophy-taking ritual performed by the killer. As it became evident that a serial killer was on the loose, fear gripped the densely populated Southern Ontario tier between Toronto and Niagara Falls, Fort Erie and Buffalo, New York just across the border. Billboards with a mysteriously sinister brown-coloured Camaro reportedly connected to the disappearance of one the girls went up around the region calling on witnesses to phone in tips as parents grounded their high school-age daughters.

When the perpetrator was identified and arrested in 1993, to everyone's shock it turned out to be two perpetrators: a young newlywed couple that might have stepped out of the pages of a supermarket checkout line wedding magazine, Paul Bernardo and Karla Homolka. They were so shiny perfect and beautiful a couple that they were dubbed the "Ken and Barbie Killers" referencing the idolized dolls that millions of girls play with. In a mutually sick and twisted pursuit of their darkest

sexual fantasies, the two not only lured, kidnapped, held captive, raped, tortured and murdered the girls before disposing of their bodies, but also recorded themselves performing their rapes on videotape. Their serial killer video selfies would become horrific courtroom evidence. While in the past, serial killers have been known to take still photographs or record audio of their victims screaming and begging for mercy, it's only in the 1980s that small portable video cameras began to be widely available for consumers. Bernardo and Homolka compulsively recorded everything on videotape, leaving behind a horrific record of exactly what organized, sadistic serial killers do to their victims. In criminal history up until then, never have homicidal videotapes as detailed and extensive as those recorded by Homolka and Bernardo been entered into evidence—not even the notorious videotapes of Leonard Lake and Charles Ng taunting and torturing their female victims in California in the mid-1980s. To everyone's shock, the couple were charged with a third murder when videos revealed they had drugged, raped and killed Karla's own little sister, Tammy, on Christmas Eve, as the parents slept upstairs, recording that rape on video. Karla would later explain that her kid sister's virginity was her "Christmas-wedding gift" to her husband-to-be, as an act of atonement for her own lack of virginity. She was later angered by the death of her sister because her parents couldn't "get

over it" and were being all Debbie-downer on her cheery wedding plans.

Making matters even more controversial, before the police got the videotapes into their possession, Paul Bernardo's attorney, Ken Murray, on his client's instructions, took them from their hiding place and concealed them for seventeen months while Karla Homolka made a deal to testify against her husband as a "battered wife" victim in exchange for a substantially reduced sentence on the premise she too was a victim. When the videotapes were finally turned over to police, they confirmed that Karla had gleefully participated in the rapes and torture of the girls, but it was too late to change the deal. Her plea bargain was locked-in. While Paul Bernardo today is locked up for the rest of his life, Karla Homolka has already been free for a decade as of this writing, having remarried (the brother of her recent attorney) and giving birth to three children. Recently, after a leisurely life in the coconuts and sunshine of the French Caribbean island of Guadeloupe raising her little darlings, Karla and her happy brood have returned to the bosom of Canada in 2014. The case of the Ken and Barbie Killers shocked, and still shocks not only Canadians, but everyone around the world to this day.

The Perfect Couple

When arrested, he was 28 and she was 22 years old. They looked Photoshopped in real life. Paul Bernardo was blond, blue-eyed, tall, athletic, intelligent, charismatic and classically handsome with what many described as an angelic baby face that made women's blood rush and pupils dilate at the mere sight of him. He was gorgeous. So was Karla with her Barbie doll head of thick shiny blonde tresses. She was brightly blue-eyed, smart, articulate, vulnerably petite with a well-proportioned knock em' dead body and wholesome central-European milk and honey good looks. He was a university-educated chartered accountant in a big prestigious downtown Toronto Bay Street firm while she was a recent high school graduate who worked as a veterinarian's assistant but really wanted to be a policewoman or a housewife. Both were brought up in anonymous, middle-middle-class suburbs, attended typically middle-middle-class suburban schools. They frequented typical high school and college student events and parties. Everything about them was "middle-middle" typical —their tastes and styles were not too high class and not too low class. They were aspiring upscale shopping-mall mediocre with ambitions for super wealth and affluence of the 'rich and famous.'

Paul and Karla were married in a lavish, but again, typically mediocre ceremony that could have, and probably did, come from the pages of a bridal

catalog. They left the church in an open horse-drawn carriage and honeymooned in Hawaii. They settled in one of those typical, wealthy, middle-sized towns that dot the fertile belt of southern Ontario known as the "Golden Horseshoe" between Toronto and Niagara Falls near the border with the United States.

They rented a perfect little lakeside Cape Cod–style house on 57 Bayview Drive in Port Dalhousie, a lakeside suburb of St. Catharines, about thirty minutes from Niagara Falls. The rent

was twelve hundred dollars a month and Karla and Paul furnished it with typical Canadian pine furniture and throw rugs. Atypically, by the time Paul and Karla left for their honeymoon, they had already raped, tortured, and murdered two adolescent girls, including Karla's younger 15-year-old sister, Tammy. So perfectly respectable, attractive, up and coming young and inoffensively middle-class was this couple that nobody dreamt of suspecting them as schoolgirls began disappearing in the region—only to be found dismembered and encased in blocks of cement by a pond or dumped naked and dead in a ditch.

Mean Girl

Karla Leanne Homolka was born in 1970 and brought up in St. Catharines, an affluent town of about 130,000 people, nestled between Toronto and Niagara Falls. The town is nicknamed the "Garden City" because of the lucrative local agricultural industries—wine grapes, apples, and vegetables. Karla was the oldest of three sisters. Her mother was Canadian—a hospital administrator. Her father emigrated from Czechoslovakia and was a dealer of lamp fixtures and black velvet paintings—the kind that feature Elvis Presley or the Beatles. Karla's father was described as a quiet 'out-of-it' non-entity

in a household dominated by four ambitious women, his wife and his three daughters.

Very little is known about Karla's home life. Her friends remember her as a bossy little girl who, with no irony intended, was called "The Princess." She had long golden blonde hair and was a very intelligent child. She had a huge collection of Barbie dolls and read children's mystery novels like Nancy Drew and the Hardy Boys. She wanted to be a detective when she grew up, she said. Her only weakness was her lack of athletic aptitude. Karla read voraciously, and her reading material during her high school years reflected a gothic taste: true crime, occult, horror, and fantasy books were among her favorites. Her childhood friends remember her as always being extremely dominant in their friendships. Many said that in high school Karla was the cleverest, prettiest, and most popular. She ruled over a pack of *Mean Girl* high school beauty princesses. They formed a little clique, calling themselves the EDC—Exclusive Diamond Club. The objective, they said, was for each member to find a rich, slightly older, good-looking man, get a diamond, marry, and live happily ever after. Karla was the dominant member of EDC. One girl would later recall, "You didn't want to get into a fight with Karla because she was going to win. She was the leader."

Yet Karla often appeared to be unhappy. Her marks slipped in high school and she seemed to be obsessed only with boys—nothing else interested

her. She desperately wanted to get married and leave school, and she went through a string of boyfriends.

When Karla was 15 and 16, she would dye her hair in garish punk shades of red and black. She was on the Pill and having sex, but so were hundreds of thousands of teenage high school girls. There were arguments at home, but nothing serious. When she was 17, she wanted to visit a boyfriend who had moved to Kansas, but her parents refused permission for her to go. She booked a flight and went anyway, but sensibly made sure to phone her parents when she arrived there to tell them she was coming back in two weeks and not to worry.

To one girl, Karla showed tiny little scratches on her wrists and said that she had attempted suicide, but the girl, who herself had seriously slashed her wrists, recalls that she did not think Karla was serious about taking her life—it was attention she wanted. There were a few dark tones to her adolescence. In one student's yearbook she wrote, "Remember: suicide kicks and fasting is awesome. Bones rule! Death Rules. Death Kicks. I love death. Kill the fucking world." Another girl recalls Karla once whispering in her ear as they sat in the school cafeteria, "I'd like to put dots all over somebody's body and take a knife and then play connect the dots and then pour vinegar all over them." Other girls remember Karla simply as a bubbly, cheerful girl who talked about going to

university and becoming a veterinarian. She worked part-time in a pet store and liked animals.

Overall, nothing dramatically traumatic has been uncovered in Karla Homolka's adolescent history that is particularly different from the lives of millions of typical teenagers. No trace of abuse, family dysfunction, rape, abandonment, or trauma. Everything was middle-middle typical.

In 1987, when Karla was 17, she and several of her friends drove to Toronto to attend a pet-store convention during a weekend. They booked into a Howard Johnson's hotel in Scarborough on Progress Road. That Friday evening, after going drinking and dancing, Karla and her friend came back to their room after midnight. They were on the make because they brought back two men with them, but it didn't work out—they sent the men on their way. Karla had changed into her pajamas and was ready for bed when she suddenly got the munchies. She called room service but was told they were already closed. However, the restaurant downstairs was still open. Karla, still dressed in her pajamas, and her friend went down to the restaurant for a late-night snack. That was the night she met Paul Bernardo.

"Bastard Child from Hell"

Hindsight can be cruel, but if there was nothing in Karla's past that signaled a potential for becoming a serial killer, everything about Paul Bernardo did. On the surface, Paul Bernardo seemed as middle-middle class typical as Karla. Paul was born in 1964, the youngest of three children. His father, Kenneth Bernardo, was a successful accountant, while his mother, Marilyn Elizabeth, was a housewife who, in her spare time, was an active Girl Guide leader. Both came from middle-class backgrounds from the prosperous rural town of Kitchener-Waterloo, located in the heart of Ontario's Mennonite farming country and home to one of the world's leading computer science universities and Blackberry. Marilyn's family

traced their high-Anglican Anglo-Saxon roots to the United Empire Loyalists—British subjects who rejected the revolution in 1776 in the Thirteen Colonies and migrated north to Canada to become the ruling elite there. What the Daughters of the American Revolution are to the United States, the United Empire Loyalists are to Canada. Marilyn's father was a prominent lawyer in Kitchener and a colonel in the Canadian Army, who had distinguished himself during the war in Italy.

Paul's father, Kenneth Bernardo, came from more humble roots. The grandfather, Frank, emigrated from northern Italy but, once in Canada, married into Anglo-Canadian stock and built a highly successful tiling company that specialized in fine marble. His son, Kenneth, grew up in Kitchener, graduated university and was eventually certified as a chartered accountant. Kenneth met Marilyn in Kitchener and it was her father, the "Colonel," who urged her to marry Kenneth because he had a university degree unlike her other suitors. After they got married, Kenneth eventually went to work for a large accounting firm in Toronto. Kenneth and Marilyn Bernardo settled in Guildwood, a wealthier neighbourhood in Scarborough, a suburb east of Toronto built during the 1950s postwar boom in Canada. Their house had a swimming pool out back, a luxury, considering that Canada's summers barely last two months.

Beneath this seemingly happy affluent family image lurked dark shadows. Kenneth beat his wife Marilyn. Her friends recall she became sullen and withdrawn after her marriage. In March 1961, they had their first child, a son, David Bryar, and in December 1962, their daughter, Deborah Gail was born. Between bouts of alternatively being ignored or beaten by her husband, tied down by two young children, in November 1963, Marilyn had an affair with a former suitor and became pregnant with Paul. He was born on August 27, 1964.

When the newborn infant Paul was brought to Marilyn's bedside, she was horrified to see a huge purple mark disfiguring his face, like something today out of a Stephen King novel or *The Omen* or *Rosemary's Baby*—a 'devil's child' mark. Doctors assured her that it was a transient natal blood clot that would fade, and indeed it did after six weeks. But it was an inauspicious start for the baby. Like many serial killers, Paul Bernardo had infant disorders and early illnesses. He suffered from a form of aphasia as a result of a lack of oxygen to the brain during birth combined with a physical deformity in the palate of his mouth. As a child he did not speak, making only animal-like sounds, until minor corrective surgery at the age of five literally loosened his tongue. For several years following, he stuttered and had speech impediments.

As a child in school, Bernardo was isolated and tormented by other children, who chanted "smelly Barnyard, dirty Barnyard." Isolation and loneliness as a child is a common trait among serial killers. It's not that loneliness makes a child into a serial killer, it's that in loneliness and rejection, the child withdraws into a world of fantasy that often involves control and revenge against the world that has rejected him, and when those fantasies of revenge and control fuse badly with a sexual impulse and masturbatory conditioning, they begin to cook and stew into a deadly brew. Add physical and/or mental trauma to the mix and that still unknown 'X' factor that psychologists and criminologists are trying to identify—i.e., why do so many abused children *not* become automatically serial killers—we begin to then approximate the psychopathological demons driving a Paul Bernardo as a sadistic serial offender.

Witnesses recalled that the Bernardos' home life was "stormy" and that husband and wife had separate bedrooms. When Paul was a child, his mother, grew obese, passive, and depressed. She was no longer feeding her children and hoarded food under her bed in her basement bedroom while the family fridge remained empty. The house was in filthy condition. When Paul was about 5 or 6 years old, he apparently ran away from home and remained absent for several days. Paul's older brother, David, said that nobody in the family even asked him where he had been.

Like Ted Bundy, Bernardo learned in late adolescence that his origins were not those he had thought they were. He was 15 or 16 when his mother after another in a series of bitter arguments with his father, burst into Paul's room and threw down on his bed a picture of a man and declared that he was Paul's real father. It was a total shock to him. Afterwards, she would refer to her son as the "bastard child from hell." Paul began referring to his mother as "bitch" and "whore." In an interview, his father confirmed that Paul was not his biological son, but said, "That's his hang-up. That's never been a hang-up with me."

When his grotesquely obese mother would come up the stairs from her dark basement bedroom where she kept the lights off and curtains drawn, his father would comment, whether they had company or not, "Boom, boom, boom, look out, here comes the big, fat cow." Paul would describe to his high school buddies how his father would creep down into the basement in the night to have sex with "it" before scurrying back to his own bedroom.

Paul's parents: Marilyn and Ken Bernardo

All this was shocking to Paul's high school friends, because by high school, Paul was well turned out: neatly dressed, preppy, handsomely attractive to girls, hardworking and reliable, rarely missing a day in school. His grades in maths and sciences were in the eighties. He was likable and personable. But a few of his friends who visited his home, later remarked on the disordered and chaotic home life and his bug-eyed crazy-haired mother lurking in the dark at the bottom of the basement stairs and the filth and disorder of the house he lived in.

It was even worse than that. When Paul was a child, his father repeatedly sexually abused Paul's sister Deborah since she was nine years old. The entire family would gather on Sunday evenings, huddled together on the couch in a darkened room to watch Walt Disney while the father fingered the little girl so roughly she would cry out in pain. The mother would gurgle from her end of the couch, "What's going on there?" but would never intervene. Deborah would have to draw the curtains in her bedroom when undressing for bed because Kenneth would climb out on the roof to watch her through the window, claiming he was inspecting the gutters in the dark. At night Kenneth would creep into her room to molest her. A heavy sleeper, Deborah took to sleeping with a barricade of nutshells and garbage cans full of coins while clutching a flashlight. When she'd be awakened by the sound of her father coming for her, she would

shine the light into her father's face in an attempt to ward him off. In a bizarre twist, on the same day that Paul Bernardo was arraigned in court after his arrest, his father, Kenneth, by then aged 58, was appearing in an adjoining courtroom for his sentencing hearing after pleading guilty to repeatedly and indecently assaulting his daughter 20 years earlier, between January 1969 and June 1974. She pressed charges as an adult after she became convinced that he was molesting her own daughter.[1]

Paul's father did not confine his psycho shit to the privacy of the family home.   A female neighbor called police after observing him while sitting in friend's car across the street, peeping into her windows while dressed in his pajamas. According to the classic FBI study of serial killers and sexual murderers, *Sexual Homicide: Patterns and Motives* (1988) by John Douglas, Robert Ressler and Ann Burgess, this places Paul into a category that 50 to 53 percent of all serial killers can be found in: parents with criminal and psychiatric records.

"Big, Bad Businessman"

Despite the sick home life, on the surface Paul grew up to be a popular and athletic youth by his high school teen years. He was remembered as a popular summer camp counselor who was very kind, gentle, and helpful to children. He worked successfully as an Amway salesman and became involved in Christian television broadcasting. He appears as an extra in a movie about cancer marathon runner Terry Fox. He was involved in counseling boy scouts. Again, everybody who remembered Bernardo from those days commented on his kind demeanor and his angelic face.

Bernardo was, however, developing a secret life. Since about the age of 10, he was collecting women's lingerie advertisements, although so were probably millions of other 10-year-old boys. But there was more to it. Some of his fantasies he was taking "out on the road" and acting them out. The neighbors caught him window-peeping several times, and on one occasion the police were called for the son like for the father. Friends recall that by the time Bernardo was in his late teens, he was an avid aficionado of pornographic videos and slasher horror movies.

When Paul was 19, he entered the University of Toronto to study accounting like his father. His girlfriend from that period later testified that he would enjoy having rough sex with her. He would take her in his car to deserted factory parking

lots, choke her with a cord, force anal sex on her, and order her to masturbate with a wine bottle. By the age of 19, he was already heavily scripting ritual rough sex.

During his college years, Bernardo began supplementing his income by smuggling tax-free cigarettes from Niagara Falls, New York, into Canada. He was developing a psychopath's double life, engaging in risky behaviour that, if exposed, threatened to bring his 'public' life crashing down. He saw himself as an "outlaw" and even when later gainfully employed as a chartered accountant in a blue-chip accounting firm, he continued his smuggling activities. It's what psychopaths live for, a desperate search for an emotional charge from taking secret life risks that threaten their otherwise emotionally flat "normal" day-to-day life. As a smuggler, Bernardo became intimately familiar with the terrain that lies between Toronto and the Falls, which would eventually become his stalking and dumping ground.

One night in October 1987, Bernardo and a friend walked into a Howard Johnson's hotel restaurant on Progress Road in Scarborough for a late-night coffee. The instant Paul laid eyes on a cute little blonde sitting at a table in her pajamas, he immediately went over to her. They chatted for about an hour, Bernardo spinning stories of his business ambitions. The 17-year-old Karla Homolka was enthralled by the handsome, aggressive, confident, blond, 23-year-old Paul; she called him

the "big, bad businessman"—like in "the big, bad wolf." Homolka and her friend invited the two men upstairs to their room. An hour later, Bernardo stripped Karla's pajamas down around her ankles and the two fell into bed while the other couple presumably fell into the other bed. Karla and Paul had mated immediately in some kind of frenzied chemistry of animal sexual lust for each other—the meeting of dark souls from the opposite poles of hell.

Paul and Karla shortly after they met, December 1987

Wives and girlfriends of sexual sadists prison study

When the Bernardo-Homolka case broke, a lot of people were shocked by this partnership of a female in serial sadistic rapes and murders. They should not have been. It actually is not all *that* rare. Almost one out of every six serial killers is a female and very frequently, the female is acting as a partner with a male.

During the mid-1930s, psychologist Abraham Maslow made a number of studies of how sexual behavior related to dominance. He noted that, in captivity, the most dominant monkeys engaged in almost constant sex, and that the nature of the sex was often "abnormal", the male monkeys sometimes mounting other males and even instances of dominant females mounting males. Maslow concluded that sex in those circumstances was an expression of dominance, rather than a primal reproductive urge. He noted that when a new monkey was introduced into the group, the lowest dominance monkeys would react with the most violence. Maslow concluded these attacks were the type of low-esteem violence noted in humans.

Maslow then turned his attention to young college girls, whom he interviewed in great detail. Maslow concluded that female sexuality is also linked to dominance. He found that people fell into

one of three categories: high-dominance, medium-dominance, and low-dominance.

High-dominance women were the most sexually active. They were promiscuous, sexually adventurous and uninhibited. Medium-dominance women tended also to be very sexual, but would usually relate to one male partner at a time. Low-dominance women had a very negative opinion of sex, engaged in it infrequently, and felt its only purpose was for reproduction. Maslow noted that the characteristics had nothing to do with sexual drive. Women in all three categories had the same level of drive, but the amount of sex that women in each category engaged in differed.

Maslow found that, in most relationships, women preferred males who were slightly more dominant than themselves but within the same dominance group. It was very rare for a woman in Maslow's survey to be interested in any male from a lower dominance group. Maslow found that most medium-dominance women found high-dominance men too frightening, and the same for low-dominance women when it came to being with medium-dominance men.

In certain situations, however, partners from different dominance groups mate, and a very severely disturbed dynamic begins to emerge. The reason often is some type of emotional or psychological disorder that leads an individual to prefer mates from a different dominance class. High-dominance individuals with personality

disorders and a need to sadistically dominate their mates may seek out partners in a lower-dominance category, while low-dominance individuals can be compelled to act out abusive scenarios by seeking out higher-category mates. The result is often a slave-like, almost hypnotic relationship between two parties, where one partner totally dominates the other, yet both are desperately dependent upon the other. Sometimes, the one vital element that a dominant partner lacks in order to unleash a homicidal fantasy is provided by the submissive partner.

In California in the late 1970s-early 1980s, Charlene Williams, a 24-year-old highly educated young woman with a tested I.Q. of 160, raised in a stable, wealthy prominent family, a talented violinist and highly motivated, one evening, while buying recreational drugs at a club, met Gerald Gallego, a convicted criminal and sex offender. Charlene was instantly attracted to Gallego's "outlaw" persona and married him.

Like Karla Homolka, Charlene was probably a high-dominance woman who needed a high-dominance man—Gerald was perfect. He fantasized, along with his bi-sexual wife Charlene about keeping virginal young sex slaves at a remote country house. On his daughter's (from another marriage) fourteenth birthday, he sodomized her and raped her friend as Charlene watched. Things went wrong when one night the both of them seduced a 16-year-old go-go dancer. The three-way

sex was fine, but the next day, after coming back from work, Gallego found Charlene and the dancer having sex without him. He became enraged, threw the girl out, and stopped having sex with Charlene. Charlene then suggested that they kidnap, rape, and murder young girls. Killing between September 1978 and November 1980, they often kidnapped girls from Sacramento shopping malls. They also killed in Nevada and Oregon, often beating in the heads of their victims with a tire iron or shooting them with a .25-caliber pistol. They buried alive one victim, a pregnant woman. In three instances, they kidnapped two women at a time. Gerald shared the victims with Charlene, who liked to bite one girl as another performed oral sex on her. She bit the nipple off one of the victims.

They were eventually apprehended after murdering ten girls they had used as sex slaves, and Gerald Gallego was sentenced to death, while Charlene Gallego, in a hauntingly prophetic turn as to what will happen with Karla Homolka, received a sixteen-year sentence in exchange for testifying against Gerald as a "battered spouse victim." While in prison, she continued her education, studying a range of subjects from psychology to business to Icelandic literature.

On July 17, 1997, Charlene was set free and reverted to her family name of Williams. In an interview, she claimed that she was as much a victim of Gallego as the other girls: "There were victims who died and there were victims who lived.

It's taken me a hell of a long time to realize that I'm one of the ones who lived."

Charlene said of Gerald Gallego, "He portrayed to my parents that he was a super family guy. But soon it was like being in the middle of a mud puddle. You can't see your way out because he eliminated things in my life piece by piece, person by person, until all I had around me were members of his family, and they're all like him, every one of them…. Prison was freedom compared to being with him."

Like Karla, Charlene now lives the good life, independently wealthy under an assumed name in Sacramento where she says she spends her free time doing charity work. In a 2013 interview, she said of the victims, "You know, I tried; I tried to save some of their lives… I tried to get away. I tried, and people, especially women, will say, 'Well, if you want to get away, you can always get away.' It's not that easy; it's not that easy at all," she said. "I don't know (why Gallego didn't kill me), because he sure tried."

Asked about her former partner in the rapes and murders, she said, "He is just one sick bastard, he was. I would've done anything I could if I could've stopped him. I know I couldn't have stopped him; I tried to stop him. I put him on death row. Am I proud of that? Yes I am."[2]

In the late 1970s, Carol Bundy (no relation to Ted Bundy) accompanied her lover, Douglas Clark, as he picked up and murdered prostitutes on

Hollywood Boulevard in Los Angeles. At one point, he severed a girl's head and brought it home. Carol washed and set the victim's hair and applied makeup to the head in order that Clark could have sex with it. Eventually Carol brutally murdered a male victim to impress Clark. In England in the 1960s, Myra Hindley and Ian Brady, "The Moors Murderers," killed five children and youths, recording one girl's rape on audio tape, and more recently, Fred and Rose Mary West tortured, raped and murdered ten victims, including their own daughter, in 1971-1987. And in the early 1950s, in the United States, we had the notorious "Honeymoon Killers," Martha Beck and Raymond Fernandez, who killed two women and a child they lured through 'lonely heart' ads in newspapers. It's not uncommon.

It's when you have a mating of two high-dominance individuals, like Karla and Paul, when one is marginally submissive, but otherwise high-dominance, that one begins to get into crazy town. In 2002, Janet Warren and veteran FBI profiler Roy Hazelwood published the results of interviews with twenty incarcerated former wives and girlfriends of sexual sadists, seven of whom participated in the killing of a total of nineteen victims.[3] Four of the women involved with murderers were actually present at the murder and were charged as accomplices, and two can be easily identified as Charlene Gallego and Karla Homolka, even though

the study does not identify the participants by their actual names.

Seventeen (85 percent) of the women in the survey were raised in an intact family and had no previous arrest histories prior to meeting their mates. The other three were arrested for minor charges: stealing a tube of lipstick at the age of fourteen, a typewriter from work, and a check from work. Seventy-five percent of the women had graduated high school or had some college education, and 50 percent were in either a skilled or professional labor category. Twenty percent were students at the time they met their partner. Only four of the women reported alcohol or drug abuse, suicide attempts, or mental health issues prior to their relationship with the sadist. The researchers concluded that the majority of these women "lived rather conventional, stable, and noncriminal lives before the initiation of the relationship that culminated in rather radical changes in their behavior." This is diametrically opposite to what we know of solo female serial killers, who tend to have unstable family histories, relatively poor academic performances, juvenile criminal records and psychiatric histories.

Other aspects of their childhood histories, however, more closely resembled those of solo female serialists and male serial killers as well. Thirty-five percent of the women reported abusive family discipline, and nearly half (45 percent) reported continual sexual abuse in their childhood;

30 percent identified their father as the abuser when they were between the age of 4 and 8. The sexual abusers included fathers, brothers, a grandmother, an aunt, a sister, and other acquaintances. There were no cases of sexual assault by strangers reported.

When asked why they became involved in abusive and sadistic relationships, 75 percent of the women replied that it was out of love and desire to please the man. Two women described themselves as extremely naïve, two indicated that they wanted to get away from home, and one could offer no explanation.

The majority of women (85 percent) stated that the men were gentle and caring when they first met them, gave them surprise gifts (65 percent), took them on trips (40 percent), and had a "great deal of money to spend on them" (85 percent). When asked why they remained in the relationship, only three of the twenty women attributed it to love; eight said they were either naïve or stupid and hoped their partner's behavior would improve; one for financial dependency and one for emotional dependency. Only seven women reported they remained out of fear of their partner.

Asked why they left the relationship, eight said out of fear for their lives; three out of fear for their children's lives; three because their partners were arrested; five for other reasons; and one was left by her partner. Fear appeared to be almost equally (35–40 percent) the motive in a large

minority of cases why the women either remained or left the relationships.

The authors of the study characterized these women as "compliant victims." They concluded that while all the women "express a willingness to exchange their compliance in return for the attention and affection of the sadistic male, there also appears to be a more subtle dynamic operative in which some of the women became assimilated into the sexual aggression of their partner." They believed that all of the women who engaged in this type of behavior did so only after meeting their partner, and in those cases where the women participated in murder, they would not have done so on their own, independent of the men. Alternatively, the authors felt the males would have murdered even if they had not met their female partner—at least in those seven cases out of the twenty.

Finally, the study concluded: "It is also our opinion that these men and their behaviors do not reflect the more extreme end of the continuum of behavior associated with 'wife batterers.' Although some men who batter their wives may also be sexual sadists, it is our impression that the majority of them are not."

Hybristophilia

Psychiatrists are still trying to unravel the exact dynamics of the relationship between Bernardo and Homolka. Karla was a dominant, smart and aggressive young woman, yet she became totally submissive to Paul. She was no doubt a high-dominance personality and believed that she needed a strong and willful man in her life. The psychopath Bernardo matched the bill. The final link in the formula was Homolka's total lack of any sense of morality. Despite her intelligence, for whatever reasons, she lacked a moral compass. (Karla was tested for psychopathy and did not score highly on the psychopathy scale, although it is possible that she was smart enough to manipulate her results.) When she came together with the psychopathic Bernardo and went along with him into his fantasies, the path to murder was laid.

If labels are needed for what is wrong with Karla, than *hybristophilia* could fit the bill, also known as the "Bonnie and Clyde syndrome." The term is derived from the Greek word ὑβρίζειν (hubrizein), meaning "to commit an outrage against someone" (which in turn is derived from ὕβρις (hubris)) and "philo", meaning "having a strong affinity or preference for." It is best described as an attraction in a female toward an aggressive, dominant, sadistic male. It's why so many women correspond with serial killers and even marry them. A *hybristophiliac* is not a masochist—seeking out

ritual and physical sexual submission—but is aroused by the sadism of her partner toward *other* victims. Some argue it's an overdeveloped primitive survival mechanism in the female brain that draws her to mate with and tame for herself the most vicious and aggressive of males in a herd to guarantee her own and her offspring's survival and dominance. It may explain why women are so frequently excited by and attracted to "bad boys" over "nice guys" and why true crime serial killer literature is so avidly read and consumed by female readers. The serial killer is the ultimate "bad boy" in that instinctual matrix that still lives on and lurks in our brains from thousands of years ago when humans lived like animal herds—a period that over the roughly one million years of humanoid existence is relatively recent—like yesterday. Out of a million years, we have been "civilized" for only about 12,000 years. (That's like 12 cents out of $100, for a sense of scale.) All sorts of violent, sexual and cannibalistic impulses previously necessary for a species to survive throughout that time, still pulsate, spark and seethe in the primitive human brain, waiting for just the right combination of socialization, trauma, environment, genetics and bio-chemistry to unleash a monster.

What makes so many of the other cases of male-female criminal partnerships different from Bernardo is that in most cases, at least one, if not two of the partners could be described as very obviously and visibly "losers" or overtly

dysfunctional. Myra Hindley was meek and stupid with low self-esteem while Ian Brady was smart and cocky but an underachiever with Nazi atrocity fantasies. Both Martha Beck and Carol Bundy were conventionally unattractive, obese with google-eyed Coke-bottle glasses, while their mates were also underachievers with evident mental health and behavioral issues.

Closest to Karla Homolka, Charlene Gallago might have come from "respectable" roots, but her partner Gerald was a convicted sex offender from a family of sex offenders. They were all dramatically dysfunctional or socially marginal before they began killing. This was not completely the case with Paul Bernardo and Karla Homolka. Even with Paul's dysfunctional family history, most people were not aware of it, and he successfully maintained a mask of a sane, productive, functioning, hardworking, attractive man making his way up the middle-class ladder of success to potentially greater and better things. Bernardo was no Ian Brady or Gerald Gallego. His mask was very well constructed and was very hard to see through because it was built on a popular consumer society cultural construct of what a "successful" young middle-class male should be aspiring to. Bernardo adopted it like a chameleon's skin. The same for Karla: a popular girl in her high school, attractive in the conventional sense, smart and ambitious, she was not the "troll" that Martha Beck, Myra Hindley or Carol Bundy were. But she was morally numb. A

suburban *Mean Girl* craving approbation. She was a Facebook 'like' slut before there was Facebook. And now these two handsomely beautiful objects of middle-class taste and values, invisibly ugly and evil on the inside, mated. Now the killing would begin.

Prince Charming

By the time Paul Bernardo arrived in St. Catharines to see Karla the following weekend after meeting her, she had told all her Exclusive Diamond Club friends that she had met her Prince Charming. He called at her home and met her parents, and then the two went out to see a movie: *The Prince of Darkness*, a horror film about the unleashing of an evil spirit into the world. Afterward, Karla had invited some of her friends to her home for a small party. All who met Bernardo agreed with Karla—he was a dream boy. During the party, Karla and Paul slipped away into her bedroom upstairs. When they closed the door, Bernardo noticed Karla's jean jacket hanging on the handle: It had a pair of handcuffs sewn to it as decoration. Karla told Paul that he could use those on her. He handcuffed her to the rails of her bed and they had sex. Friends of Karla's remarked that she kept a sexy lingerie teddy hanging in her room with a pair of handcuffs intertwined with it, and that might have been *before* she met Bernardo.

Paul was charming and bright around her parents and appeared to be an attentive boyfriend. He called Karla his "Little Princess." He would visit every weekend and Wednesday, bringing flowers and gifts. Homolka would always be ready for him with a syrupy-sweet little note. Hundreds of these notes would be entered into evidence later at his murder trial. After some time, Homolka convinced

her parents to allow Paul to spend the night at their house on the couch, so that they could spend more time together during his visits from Scarborough. During the night, Paul would sneak up to Karla's bedroom for hot muffled furtive sex under her covers and make his way back down to the couch before her parents got up.

Karla soon became aware that her Prince Charming seemed to want to have less vaginal sex with her and preferred that she fellate him instead. Whenever they had vaginal sex, Bernardo seemed to be unable

to climax and appeared bored and distracted. They would drive to a popular fishing location, Lake Gibson, and there Bernardo would have Karla perform fellatio on him in the car. Early in their relationship, one night at her house, Karla witnessed Bernardo sneak out into the night and go around the back of the house to watch her 12-year-old sister, Tammy, undressing to go to bed. It was the beginning of Paul's obsession with Tammy.

Scarborough Rapist

In December 1987, two months *after* he met Karla, Bernardo committed what is thought to be his first of a series of extremely brutal and violent rapes in Scarborough. Between May of 1987 and December of 1992, Bernardo raped or sexually assaulted at least eighteen women in Scarborough, Peel Region, and St. Catharines and, in tandem with Karla Homolka, killed at least three women in St. Catharines and Burlington.

The rapes were every woman's worst-case scenario nightmare: The victims often got off the bus near their home late at night. They were jumped or "blitzed" from behind by a stranger from the dark, dragged out of view behind bushes, forced face down on the ground and ordered to keep their eyes closed as they were beaten, raped, and sodomized viciously. In the first several cases, the rapist failed to successfully penetrate the victim, but as his crimes escalated and as he became more comfortable with his attacks, the later victims were vaginally and anally raped and forced to perform oral sex. The beatings escalated as well. One of the later victims had her collarbone broken.

Toronto Police launched a massive operation to apprehend the serial rapist and even turned to the FBI's Behavioral Science Unit for advice. Just how 'hit and miss' FBI profiling can be is evident from the report the FBI submitted to the Toronto Police:

Your offender is a white male, 18 to 25 years of age… we believe your offender lives in the Scarborough area. He is familiar with Scarborough, especially the initial assault sites, and, therefore, in all probability lives in the immediate vicinity of those first assaults. The offender's anger towards women will be known by those individuals who are close to him.

He will speak disparagingly of women in general conversation with associates. He is sexually experienced but his past relationships with women have been stormy and have ended badly. In all probability he has battered women he has been involved with in the past. He places the blame for all his failures on women. If he has a criminal record, it will be one of assaultive behaviour. The arrests will likely be for assault, disturbing the peace, resisting arrest, domestic disturbance, etc. His aggressive behaviour would have surfaced during adolescence. His education background will be at the high school level with a record of discipline problems. He may have received counselling for his inability to get along with others, his aggressiveness, and or substance abuse. He is bright, but an underachiever in a formal academic setting. He is nocturnal and spends

a good deal of time on foot in the target assault area.

We believe your offender is single. The offender has an explosive temper and can easily become enraged. This rage transfers over into the rest of his life. He blames everyone else for his problems.

His work record will be sporadic and spotty as he cannot hold a job due to his inability to handle authority. He is financially supported by his mother or other dominant female in his life. He is a lone wolf type of person. He can deal with people on a superficial level but prefers to be alone.

Paul Bernardo's name as a possible suspect was first raised in police correspondence in January 1988, after the fifth rape in Scarborough. A woman contacted a personal acquaintance who was a police officer asking for advice on how to recover money she had loaned to Bernardo. After informally speaking with her, the Toronto Police officer filed the following report to the Scarborough Rape Task Force:

METROPOLITAN TORONTO POLICE SUPPLEMENTARY REPORT
SEXUAL ASSAULT   22 Jan 1988
Possible Suspect: Paul Kenneth
BERNARDO, 24 yrs. 21 Sir Raymond Dr., (Guildwood & Galloway) M/W, 6", 180 lbs., light brown collar length hair, clean shaven,

mole under nose, slightly crooked nose, ukn. eyes, no accent; no scars/tattoo. wears: right hand gold ring with 3 diamonds; possibly a high school ring with red stone. drives: white capri unk. lic. knife: stiletto type (blade not folding) in dark leather case
Info from: Sgt. McNiff 2753 of 52 Division (Island Station) local 2035 …
VIA–[I. F.], 18 yrs., [address, telephone number]

Ms. [F.] is a daughter of friends, and as a result of the information detailed in the following supplementary, asked to see the writer to obtain advice. Her desire was to learn how to end the relationship, and to get some money back that was owed. It was the writer who linked the a/m person to being a suspect to the sexual assaults, rather than any revenge factor in Ms. [F.]

NOTE: details are sketchy–the writer was not taking notes and was not speaking to Ms. [F.] from the point of view of a police officer.

In the early part of 1987, [I. F.] met and started dating Bernardo. They had a normal relationship, with probably sexual relations though this was not stated by [F.]

Bernardo is described as manipulative and aggressive. His behaviour progressed from gesturing to slap her in a joking manner, to threatening to do so, to giving her light taps, which became harder and harder.

On at least one occasion in November, when they were in his car, he wanted her to have sex with him. He pulled out the knife, and wanted to have an orgasm while he held it to her throat: she states she did not have sex with him this way.

In late November, the two were out for the evening, and on the way home, he drove to an isolated factory area. He had been smacking her, and yelling at her. They had an argument, and Ms. [F.] wanted to leave the car, but he wouldn't let her. He worked himself into a frenzy, and was looking for the knife, but didn't find it. At one point, he started talking to himself, and banging his head on the steering wheel saying: "Why do I do this, why?" She got out the car and hid from him. He spent some time looking for her, making promises and threats. She wandered until she found the home of a friend. This was the last time she saw the man. (Prior to the final escape, she had gotten away once, he had caught her,

punched and kicked her and rolled her in the mud bringing her back to the car.)

On an earlier occasion, Bernardo had driven [F.] and her girlfriend to a house in Markham, the home of the Van Smirnoffs. The girls were taken to the basement of the home, where two other young men were waiting: the girls thought they were going to a party. It is this officer's opinion that the men had the intention of having group sex. It was only that the girls wanted to get out (despite threats and assault) and the fact the mother of the house was awoken that this did not occur.

Ms. [F.] asked this officer for advice. Despite having been taken to Scarborough General twice for injuries, she did not want charges laid. Her main desire was to have money returned to her she had lent to Bernardo; further she was afraid he would come back and force himself on her. To date, he has not done so.

For purposes of your enquiries, from Ms. F..'s statements, the parents Bernardo and Van Smirnoffs do not seem like normal parents in that they allow things to go on in their home that normal parents would not. Bernardo is negative on CNI, CPIC, MANNIX. [Police databases.]

Toronto Police sergeant McNiff's gut feeling that Bernardo was a perfect suspect candidate was bang-on 100 percent correct. But this was 1988 and Toronto Police still routinely worked on paper, not in the electronic digital domain. His report was just another piece of paper in a mountain of paper that needed to be carefully read, remembered, filed and prioritized. There were no easily available computers for analysis and case management, nor easily shareable data platforms.

The report landed on somebody's desk, was filed away and promptly forgotten. As one investigator later said, "Back then everything was on paper. It was a paper driven process. There was paper everywhere. It was a nightmare. There were walls and walls of stuff."

Had police followed up on the report and took a closer look at Bernardo in 1988, Tammy Homolka, Leslie Mahaffy and Kristen French would still be alive today, women in their forties, probably mothers with children. But the McNiff report was filed away and forgotten.

"Your little girl wants to be abused"

In the meantime, Bernardo was letting his true sexual colour emerge with his 17-year-old girlfriend, Karla. He now ordered her to call herself disparaging names when she performed fellatio: "'cocksucker,' 'cunt,' and 'slut.'" They had to be in that precise order. In the car at Lake Gibson, Karla would have to say as she began fellating him, "My name is Karla. I am 17. I'm your little cocksucker. I'm your little cunt. I'm your little slut."

Bernardo's rape victims reported that he had demanded that they comply with a similar script.

Then in December, Bernardo announced that since Karla was not a virgin when they met, they should have anal sex. Karla refused and this became a source of stress in their relationship for the next two months. Bernardo demanded that Karla invent a name for his penis. She came up with "Snuffles." A letter sent by Karla to Paul included a love coupon, which stated: "The bearer will receive one cute little blonde 17-year-old to put on her knees between his legs and satisfy his wishes." In an accompanying note, Karla wrote:

Dear Paul,
You're a dream come true. You are the best, my Big, Bad, Businessman. I've been fantasizing what playful things to do with your body all day. Your strong chest. Your muscular arms. Your beautifully shaped legs. Your hard, flat stomach. And Snuffles, oh wonderful Snuffles. The pleasure I get from touching, from licking, from sucking Snuffles, is indescribable. You know what I love? Having you stick it inside me and making me gasp for air while my parents are in the next room. I love it when you shoot it into my mouth. I want to swallow every drop, and then some. The power you wield over me is indescribable. When we sit

together on the couch I have to use all my strength to keep from ripping off your clothes. You make me so horny… I love you an amount I never thought possible. Words can't even come close to expressing my feelings. With you in my life, I feel complete. Whole. With you by my side nothing can go wrong. You have opened my eyes to a new way of thinking and being. I will love you forever, no matter what.

Karla XOXOXO

In the car at Lake Gibson, Karla was then expected to follow this script: "I love having Snuffles in my mouth." "And what are you?" "Your little cocksucker." "What else?" "Your little cunt. Your slut. I want to suck on Snuffles all the time."

In February 1988, after Paul Bernardo threatened to drop her, Karla finally agreed to anal sex. He brought Karla back to his parents' house while they were away on vacation. As usual, by the time Karla had agreed to anal intercourse, Bernardo was ahead of her. Now he wanted to take pictures as well. Setting up his Polaroid camera, he had Karla masturbate with a wine bottle. He then had her get on the bed and he penetrated her anally. At one point, he tied a black electrical cord around her neck and yanked on it. In his hand, he held an eight-inch-long hunting knife. He told Karla not to worry, that the two props excited him more. The dated photographs were later entered into evidence.

Instead of running as far away from Bernardo as fast as she could, Karla actually became excited by these games and told Paul she hoped that he would marry her. In the autumn of 1988, about a year after they had met, Homolka said that Bernardo struck her for the first time. He told her he wanted her to wear a dog collar, and when she laughed, he slapped her. The next time they had anal sex, Karla was tugging on a dog leash while Bernardo tenderly whispered, "You're my little mutt." That was shortly followed by Bernardo's demand for analingus and that Karla now also add "ass-licker" to her vocabulary of scripted words. In one of Homolka's cards to Bernardo (which she wrote and mailed almost every day), she wrote— around their first anniversary.

> Thanks for the best year of my life. You enriched my life beyond belief...I want to suck Snuffles and get him so hard that he can't take it anymore. And then I want to ease your pulsating penis into my tight little cunt. Your little girl wants to be abused. She needs her Big Bad Businessman to dominate her the best he can.
> Love, Kar

In 1989, Karla Homolka graduated from high school. She wanted to become a police officer and was planning to enter the Faculty of Criminology at the University of Toronto. Bernardo

told her that he did not want "his wife" working in a job that dangerous. Thus instead of university studies, Homolka went to work as an assistant in a veterinarian's office in St. Catharines. She had thought first of going to Toronto, but by then Bernardo was on the brink of quitting his job and taking up smuggling cigarettes almost full-time. He told her that he wanted to live in the St. Catharines area, conveniently in the middle between the U.S. border and Toronto.

After the case broke, friends all unanimously recall that Karla and Paul during this period appeared to be a happy and a loving couple with a familiar today *Fifty Shades Of Grey* kinky side: love cuffs and collars. But there was no sense that Karla was an abused partner; she appeared happy in and out of his presence and there were no visible signs of anything amiss in their relationship. Even Karla herself would later say to police that she and Bernardo had argued over "typical" things a few times but that otherwise they were happy in the beginning. Before they started raping and killing.

Deadly Innocence

During Karla's high school graduation party, Bernardo displayed another side of himself. He drunkenly accused some of her fellow male students of flirting with Karla and got into a fight with several of them. Although they were members of the school football team and were quite athletic, Bernardo showed no fear in fighting them. Despite being outnumbered by big football players and receiving a few blows that bloodied his nose, Bernardo continued to throw punches and seemed to enjoy the confrontation. Unlike many serial killers, Bernardo was not afraid or physically meek in the presence of other males.

Bernardo wanted to produce a rap record and recorded an album he titled *Deadly Innocence* in his home studio. During his trial, the judge refused to allow the lyrics of the songs to be entered into evidence. In the eyes of the law, the poetry or lyrics that one writes do not necessarily reflect the actual state of mind of the artist. Perhaps…but here is what Bernardo wrote anyway:

> You think I'm innocent?
> But behind this I'm packing a lot of deadliness
> So come at, come at me
> I got a fucking nice face
> I look like a pretty boy
> Why don't you come at me, man?

Take your best shot
See what happens to you, pal
You're outta here, man
You come at me with your beer belly
And you think you're really tough
I come back, looking like I'm 13
years old
I'll kick your ass
I'll kill your parents
I'll shoot your girlfriend
And fuck your wife
That's me, Deadly Innocence.

Bernardo was as completely aware of the angelic image he projected as he was of the violent rage that seethed inside. Karla's parents and her younger sister, Tammy, were enthralled with the baby-faced Paul Bernardo. Her mother referred to him as her "weekend son," while 15-year-old Tammy was in love with her sister's boyfriend. All this time as he lusted after their younger daughter and snuffled their oldest daughter in their house, outside their house, he was viciously battering and raping vaginally, anally and orally random women he stalked on the streets.

"It was like 2,000 other calls"

Bernardo raped his fifteenth victim in the spring of 1990 in Scarborough. This time though, he made a mistake. The victim saw his face and police issued a composite sketch of the suspect that was almost a photographic likeness of Paul Bernardo. It triggered several people who knew Paul Bernardo to contact the Toronto Police.

Tammy Homolka was still alive when the police received this report

METROPOLITAN TORONTO POLICE
SUPPLEMENTARY REPORT
Date of this Report
27 Jun 1990 1300

<u>Info from:</u> Ms M… Royal Bank, Ellesmere Road & Neilson Road

The above party called S/Insp. J.Wolfe at the S.A.S. office and gave the following info.

One Paul BERNARDO 21 Sir Raymond Drive West Hill DOB 27 Aug 64 is a dead ringer for the photo in the papers of the Scarb. Rapist.

The caller also reports that he had not been seen at the Bank since the last rape until June 27/90. When seen on June 27/90 he had changed his hair style, the caller also reported that this party was a student at the Scarbor. Campus of the U. of T. and that he looks about 21/2 yrs. old.

P.C. Buchanan #1897

Suspects were being graded A, B, C, by how good of a suspect they were. By now the police were computerizing their system but many of the old school cops were scoffing at computer technology. P.C. (police constable) Buchanan would later explain why the tip was filed away and forgotten, saying, "I picked up the phone because no one else was around. The info would go into the stack and the reader would file it ABC and the criteria was did he live in Scarborough, look alike, so he ends up in the A box. Detective Sergeant gets the tip and it is given to an investigative team. It should be marked on the super duper computer

when it is cleared. We waited for the "spit" samples. If they were a non–secretor, then we go out and get blood. It was like 2,000 other calls."

An independent review of the Bernardo case, after it was all over, concluded that "By October 25, 1990 there were about 930 suspects... Detective Irwin of the Metro Sexual Assault Squad in January of 1993 referred to a number of suspects in the range of 3,000. Because there was no consistent case management system it is impossible to know exactly how many suspects there eventually were."[4]

In September 1990, four months before Tammy's murder, Alex and Tina Smirnis, a couple acquainted with Bernardo, after seeing the composite sketch of the Scarborough Rapist suspect, approached the police. Alex had grown up with Bernardo and hung out with him until he married Tina. They brought some home wedding videos and photographs of Bernardo. The Toronto Police notes from that interview read

Police notes on BERNARDO

- Alex Smirnis grew up with Paul Bernardo
- very close family friends with Alex's family
- grew up with each other in Guild
- Paul does/has done some accounting for Alex's family–family restaurant

- Alex and Paul known each other since birth
- distinctive voice
- photo & video from their wedding [Smirnis wedding]
- 24 Sir Raymond
- 21 Sir Raymond
- lives with parents
- engaged–relocating to St. Catharines
- relocating is out of Paul's nature & sudden …
- New Years Eve–1987–I…–Morningside/Lawrence (s/e) `swatted her'–said guys I want some privacy–might have beaten the shit out of her
- always young girlfriends–small petite–not bright
- Fiancé–18 years old–still in school
- started dating more than one girl–was dating an oriental girl from U of T and in his home with another girl (I…)
- Sept. 1987–oriental broke Paul's windows (occurrence on file)
- Carla–current girlfriend–met at Howard Johnson's on Progress–first night they slept together
- Paul always wanted a pure wife–his morals have gone by the wayside

- Carla says that if you wanted to know anything about girls–ask Paul–he knows
- Paul has said to Alex's brother about raping girls–out driving around and commented about getting the girl walking along the street and raping her
- Carla–2–2 1/2 years together–short, petite, light coloured hair–subservient
- dated another girls while dating Carla
- Paul–sly–manipulative–trendy–preppy dresser
- Cars–Capri, white, 1980–81 (parents) Ken Bernardo (father)
- instigator
- braggart
- talk about having sex in his suit with his briefcase in his hand–and his wife in house clothing
- very domineering
- rough sex–had joint relationship with sisters–Paul talked about having anal sex a few times
- not into conventional sex
- carries a knife in a car
- didn't like people going in his room
- at one point involved in Christian Broadcasting on TV
- scouts

- interest in money & girls
- extended credit
- leather jackets
- photos–4 years ago in red sweater
- 3 years ago in wedding
- 14 months ago–video
- Spring '87–professional worm picker at night
- 240SX Gold–since '89 leased
- past 1/2 years accounting
- insecure
- non–smoker
- left handed?
- drinks to fit in
- Florida: Mar. '89–girl passed out–taken up to room
- Paul raped her while she was passed out
- A's brother walked in on him. He said wait, he'd be done in a minute–then they could jump on (Van Smirnis & Gus)

The Scarborough Rapist Task Force had been puzzling over the sudden halt to the rapes in May 1990. The report that Bernardo had "relocated to St. Catharines" should have rung more bells than it did. Nevertheless the police now finally made a move. Two months later.

In November 1990 Paul Bernardo was invited in for an interview with the police. He came

in on November 20, cooperative but nervous. Detectives Steve Irwin and John Munro interviewed him and filed the following report.

> On Tuesday, November 20, 1990 at about 4:30 p.m., the undersigned interviewed Paul BERNARDO re the Sexual Assault on [R. L.]
>
> BERNARDO lives with his parents at 21 Sir Raymond Dr. in Guildwood Village. He stated that he has lived there for the last 24–25 years. He went to Sir Wilfred Laurier High School in the Guildwood Village.
>
> He is currently engaged to one Karla HOMOLKA 20 yrs. of age. He plans to move to St. Catharines Ontario with HOMOLKA within a month. He and HOMOLKA have just recently started a Self Development Company. Prior to this he worked in the accounting field with Price Waterhouse Co. When the undersigned asked him why his name would come up in the Scarborough Rapist case, he said that he felt that he looked like the composite drawing, and that he had a baby face like the drawing.
>
> He could not remember specifically what he was doing on the weekend of [R. L.]'s assault, but believed that he was most likely

with his girlfriend. He has been going out
with Karla HOMOLKA for the past 3 years.
BERNARDO very willingly supplied hair
samples for PGM, a blood sample and a
saliva sample. He appeared very nervous
during the interview but was very co–
operative. Samples to be submitted to CFS
[Centre for Forensic Sciences] on Nov.
21/90
Munro Det. 2245

The taking of a blood sample, instead of just saliva
samples was unusually thorough and more than
what was normally sampled from suspects on first
pass. When Munro was later asked why he decided
to ask Bernardo for a blood sample, he said, "I am
not certain. Whether it was his behaviour, or his
face being familiar to the composite. Steve [his
partner] didn't have any problems that I asked for it.
It was a combinations of things."

Samples of Bernardo's blood, hair, and
saliva were first submitted to the Centre of Forensic
Studies (CFS) on November 21, 1990. Bernardo
was one of 92 suspects whose samples were
submitted to CFS but only one of 5 for whom police
requested further DNA testing. Before CFS could
do the DNA testing, in those days, they first had to
determine whether Bernardo's serology had the type
of profile that would allow for DNA testing. That
test returned a positive result only on December 13,

1990. Police then put in a request for full DNA testing.

DNA testing even today is a painstaking process that cannot be completed overnight. Had the CFS made DNA testing of Bernardo's samples their foremost and only priority, they could have processed the testing sometime in early January, about a month later, and there would have been a positive DNA match to Bernardo in four of the Scarborough rape cases. No matter what, it would have been too late for Tammy who only had eleven days left to live, but not too late to have saved Leslie Mahaffey and Kristen French.

But it was not made a priority. The CFS DNA lab had only been first set up in the summer of 1990 and was undergoing growing pains. It was heavily backlogged with requests for DNA reports and there was no priority system implemented. The DNA sample that police requested in December 1990 would not come back from CFS with a result until February 1, 1993, over two years later!

The "Christmas Wedding Present"

In the winter of 1990, Paul Bernardo and Karla Homolka had become engaged to be married. They began to plan their wedding for June of 1991. Bernardo, in the meantime, was obsessed with Karla's little sister Tammy. He would enter her room at night while she was sleeping and masturbate on her pillow. He began to demand that Karla dress in Tammy's clothes and developed a new script for her. ("Scripting" is a typical trait of a sexually sadistic offender.) Now Karla had to say, "I'm your 15-year-old virgin. I love you. You're the king." While Karla would perform oral sex on Bernardo, he'd stare at a photograph of Tammy. He would insist that he and Karla have sex in Tammy's bedroom while she was out. None of this seemed to offend Karla and she went along with the game.

Sometime in 1990, Bernardo bought a new video camcorder. He said they would need it for the wedding. Bernardo began to obsessively record everything on videotape. One day, Bernardo and Tammy drove over to the U.S. to buy some liquor without Karla. On the way back, they stopped and necked. Karla somehow became aware of this and lashed out angrily at Bernardo: "She's a virgin. She wouldn't know what to do with Snuffles." Bernardo charged into the opening that Karla had inadvertently made: "Maybe I should have sex with Tam and teach her the proper way. Wouldn't it be

great if Tam got to feel Snuffles inside of her? Wouldn't it be great if I took her virginity?"

Karla's kid sister, Tammy

Homolka testified that she at first refused to entertain the idea, but as with Bernardo's demands for anal sex, her refusal strained their relationship. Homolka became afraid that the June wedding might not take place despite the $4,500 engagement ring Bernardo had given her. Finally, Homolka gave in toward December of 1990—she agreed to give Tammy's virginity to Bernardo as a "Christmas wedding present" as compensation for not being a virgin herself.

Karla stole some halothane, an ether-like inhalational anesthetic, from the veterinarian clinic where she worked. Then, telling a pharmacist she was ordering sedatives for the animal clinic, she also ordered some Halcion, a powerful triazolam benzodiazepine class sleeping sedative.

Sex, death, and videotape

On Christmas Eve of 1990, Bernardo and his video camera showed up at the Homolka's house to spend the holidays. Years later, television audiences would be horrified by the home videos of 15-year-old Tammy drinking down eggnog spiked with Halcion while Bernardo and Karla hovered over her, encouraging her off camera to drink up. She had less than a few hours left to live. At the end of the evening, the parents retired to bed and told Tammy she should turn in as well. Little Tammy protested: Karla and Paul had invited her to stay up with them and watch a movie on the VCR and spend some time together. The parents went to bed while Paul and Karla slid a cassette into the VCR.

The movie was *Lisa*, about a teenage girl's infatuation with a stranger that, unknown to her, is a serial killer. By the time the movie ended, Tammy had passed out from all the Halcion she had consumed. Karla quickly ran to her room and got the halothane. She poured it onto a cloth and held it around Tammy's face to make sure she was now deeply sedated into unconsciousness.

Bernardo meanwhile unbuttoned Tammy's blouse and fondled her breasts. Karla stripped naked while Bernardo pulled off Tammy's track pants and underwear. He then switched on the video camera. This part of the videotape was never broadcast on television, but it was shown to the jury in the courtroom five years later at Bernardo's trial for

murder. The prosecution transcripts of the tapes presented in court reveal what took place as recorded by Bernardo's video camera:

(Video recording starts.)
HOMOLKA: Put on a condom.
(Bernardo vaginally penetrates Tammy Homolka.)
HOMOLKA: Paul, hurry up.
BERNARDO: Shut up!
HOMOLKA: Please, hurry up, before someone comes down.
BERNARDO: Shut up. Keep her down.
(Homolka pours more halothane onto the cloth pressed against Tammy's face. Bernardo again enters Tammy. Homolka urges Bernardo to put on a condom.)
HOMOLKA: Put something on.
BERNARDO: Shut up, Karla.
HOMOLKA: Put something on. Do it.
BERNARDO: You're getting all worked up.
HOMOLKA: Fucking do it. Just do it.
(Bernardo penetrates Tammy anally. He continues for about a minute.)
BERNARDO: Do you love me?
HOMOLKA: Yes.
BERNARDO: Will you blow me?
HOMOLKA: Yes.
BERNARDO: Suck on her breasts.
HOMOLKA: I can't.

BERNARDO: Suck on her breasts. Suck. Suck. Suck.

(Homolka sucks Tammy's breasts.)

HOMOLKA: Hurry up, please.

BERNARDO: Lick her cunt.

(Bernardo pushes Homolka's head between Tammy's legs.)

BERNARDO: Lick. You're not doing it.

HOMOLKA: I am so.

BERNARDO: Do it. Lick her cunt. Lick it. Lick it up clean. Now put your finger inside.

HOMOLKA: I don't want to.

BERNARDO: Do it now. Quick, right now. Put three fingers right inside.

HOMOLKA: No.

BERNARDO: Put it inside. Inside! Inside!

(Homolka inserts her finger into Tammy's vagina. When she withdraws her finger it is glistening with dark menstrual blood.)

BERNARDO: Okay, taste it. Taste it. Inside…inside.

HOMOLKA: I did, I…did!

BERNARDO: Now do it again, deeper. Inside. Deeper. Right inside. Okay, taste good? Taste good?

HOMOLKA: Fucking disgusting!

(The video recording stops.)

Homolka later testified that at this point Bernardo struck her and told her to be more cooperative before the camera. Bernardo then switched the

68

camera back on and had Karla hold it while he again had vaginal and anal sex with Tammy. He had not climaxed when the video recorded him suddenly stopping and withdrawing. Homolka put the camera down and switched it off.

Karla testified that Bernardo said that something seemed wrong—it appeared like Tammy wasn't breathing. Tammy was dead. She had vomited and choked to death during the rape. They attempted artificial respiration but Tammy remained unresponsive. They hurriedly dressed Tammy and carried her into a bedroom and then Karla flushed the remaining Halothane down the toilet and hid the Halothane bottle, the cloth, and the Halcion container in the basement shelves near the laundry room. Then they called 911.

Police photo of the scene of Tammy's rape and death.

69

The emergency crews had arrived at the house at about 1:25 a.m. that night, but there was nothing they could do. She arrived at the local hospital at 1:45 a.m. and was pronounced dead at 2:03 a.m.

A police officer, who responded to the call, remembered seeing strange, huge, burn-like cherry red marks around Tammy's mouth, nose and face. He noted that Tammy had been moved from the living room to a bedroom. Bernardo said they had moved Tammy because the light was better in the bedroom—they could see better there. The police officer checked the lights in both rooms and saw that they were equally bright, but then thought that people under stress can react in all manner of inexplicable ways.

When asked about the red marks on Tammy's face, Bernardo replied that they probably were caused by the rug when they dragged Tammy to the other room. They would have had to drag her face down to produce those marks, the police officer thought, which was odd. But the officer's duties were to merely file the response report and not to investigate the accident. Moreover, he was a rookie who had just come on the job. He kept his suspicions to himself and left it to the senior detectives and coroner to investigate.

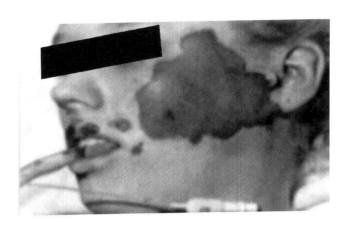

Halothane anesthetic burns on Tammy's face

Karla later claimed that Bernardo took the tape out of the camera and hid it behind a jar of pickles in the basement before the police arrived. Bernardo claims that the tape remained in the camera and, after they returned from the police station, that Karla took the tape out of the camera and hid it in her bedroom between the bed and the wall. It would be a "he said-she said" kind of thing throughout the whole case.

After the police interviewed the parents and were told that Paul Bernardo was a fine, upstanding young chartered accountant, who was scheduled to marry Karla in June and who was loved by the family like a son, the police developed no strong suspicion of him.

Forensic pathology is as much an interpretive art as it is a science. The extent to

which a pathologist will explore a death in an autopsy depends upon the external circumstances presented to him by the police. Had Tammy's body been found abandoned by a roadside, perhaps the autopsy would have been more extensive, but Tammy's body was found by her concerned, loving sister and future brother-in-law. Tests were made for illicit drugs, but the recreational kind—not for veterinary sedatives and anesthetics. The dramatic burn stains around her mouth and face, the pathologist concluded, were the result of acidity in her vomit.

Her rectum and vagina were inspected, but not carefully enough to detect indications of rape. Bernardo had not had time to ejaculate or couldn't. (Many serial killers are unable to ejaculate during their crime and are capable of reaching a climax only later, when masturbating and reliving their murder, often touching or rubbing totems and trophies like their victim's clothing, hair, sometimes body parts, or photos and videos of the victim.) Again, even if no seminal fluids were found, Tammy's vagina and anus should have been dilated enough to signal the pathologists that something was wrong, had they been looking for such signals. But they were not. The official autopsy result was death by aspiration of vomit. An accident.

During Bernardo's trial five years later, Homolka was cross-examined about her role in the death of her little sister:

Q: The first time he mentioned having sex with your sister I would have thought you'd spring out of bed and say, 'There's no way I'm going to let you touch my baby sister.' Wouldn't that be the right reaction?

A: Yes.

Q: But you didn't do that?

A: No, I didn't.

Q: You thought, 'Knock her out and have some sex with her. What's the harm'?

A: I didn't know her safety would be in danger. I was afraid he would do it regardless. I was afraid he would just grab her off the street and rape her. This was the best way. I had no choice...I thought it would happen once and it would be over.

"I loved it when you fucked my little sister"

Homolka claimed that because of Tammy, Bernardo now had something to hold over her head. She insisted that because she feared Bernardo would expose her role in Tammy's death to her parents, she became his unwilling slave. Homolka claimed that after the death of her sister, she "was numb." Obviously not numb enough to complain that her parents spent too much money on Tammy's funeral in a letter to a friend:

> My wedding plans are great, except for my parents being such assholes. They pulled out half of the money from the wedding saying they couldn't afford it. Bullshit!!! Now Paul and I have to pay for seven or eight thousand dollars of the wedding. We've been compromising like crazy; a cash bar, no flowers on the table, etc. Finally Paul and I said fuck it! No paying for the bar. Cocktails. Everything!!!
>
> Fucking parents. They are being so stupid. Only thinking of themselves. My father doesn't even want us to have a wedding. He thinks we should just go to the hall. Screw that! If he wants to sit at home and be miserable, he's welcome to it. He hasn't worked, except for one day, since

Tammy died. He's wallowing in his own misery, and fucking me. It sounds awful on paper, but I know you really see what I'm saying.

Tammy always said she wanted a Porsche on her sixteenth birthday. Now my dad keeps saying, "I should have bought it." Bull! If he really felt like that he'd be paying for my wedding because I could die tomorrow, or next year. He's such a liar. And for the real reason we moved out. My parents told Paul and I that they wanted him to stay at the house until the wedding. Then they said they wanted him to go after Tammy died because they needed their privacy. First they took away half the wedding money, and then they kicked us out. They knew how much we needed to be together, but they didn't care. What assholes!!!

A week after Tammy's death, Karla wrote Paul in January 1991.

I loved it when you fucked my little sister. I loved it when you fucked Tammy. I loved it when you took her virginity. You're the King. I love licking your ass, Paul. I bet Tammy would have loved to lick your ass. I loved it when you put Snuffles up her ass. I felt proud. I felt happy. I felt horny. It's my

death while Karla's other sister went to stay with friends. Karla and Paul were alone in the house. Bernardo spent a lot of time masturbating to the videotape they had made of Tammy's rape. He and Karla went into Tammy's room, which had remained untouched since her death. Bernardo set the video camera up on a tripod facing Tammy's bed. While Homolka put on Tammy's clothes, Bernardo warned her, "Remember, don't say anything stupid that will ruin the tape." He was still mad at Karla for saying she was not enjoying performing oral sex on her sister the night she died. Paul told her, "It's my only tape of Tammy and you fucked it up."

(Video recording starts.)
(Bernardo is lying naked on Tammy's bed. Homolka is with him, with her hair brushed forward over her face. Bernardo is holding a picture of Tammy. Homolka is performing fellatio on him.)
BERNARDO: Here's my little virgin Tammy. Fucked by me. I broke the hymen.
HOMOLKA: Tammy was a virgin.
(Bernardo turns over onto his hands and knees while Homolka performs analingus while rubbing his penis at the same time.)
HOMOLKA: I love licking your ass. I love sucking your cock. I love you. I love to be fucking you so much. (Bernardo rolls over

on his back and adjusts Homolka's hair so it covers her face. She is fellating him.)

HOMOLKA: I love you so much.

BERNARDO: I love you too, Tammy.

HOMOLKA: I want your cock in me. I'll give you the best orgasm of all. Together we're perfect. I want to lose my virginity to you.

BERNARDO: You didn't know I was filming you, Tammy, when you were in your room, undressing. But I was watching you through the window.

HOMOLKA: Can you ever stop thinking of me? Can you ever stop coming in my face? Take my virginity, Paul. Take it.

BERNARDO: I will, Tammy. I love you, Tammy. (Bernardo positions Homolka on her hands and knees and enters her anally. He is still holding Tammy's photograph in his hand.)

HOMOLKA: Oh, I'm losing my virginity. I love you, Paul. I love you so much. (Bernardo repositions the video camera at the side of the bed. He motions to Homolka to enter the frame while he looks directly into the camera.)

BERNARDO: Hi, Tam.

HOMOLKA: Hi, Paul.

BERNARDO: Gonna make me happy?

HOMOLKA: I love sucking you.

BERNARDO: You're better than Karla, that's for sure.
HOMOLKA: I love you. Will you fuck me, Paul?
(While Homolka performs oral sex, Bernardo holds the picture of Tammy.)
HOMOLKA: I'm a virgin.
BERNARDO: Oh, Tammy. Oh, I love you. Yes. Yes. Yes, my little virgin. Yes.
HOMOLKA: I love you, Paul. I'm your virgin.
(Homolka performs fellatio on Bernardo for twenty minutes until he climaxes.) (Video recording stops.)

The next night Bernardo went out driving. Before leaving, he told Homolka that if he came back with a girl, she was to hide or pretend to be his sister. He returned with a young woman about 16 years old and the two had sex while Homolka hid behind the drapes. The next night, Bernardo made another tape. This one was made by a roaring fireplace in the same room where Tammy had died. Bernardo was stretched out on his back with a glass of wine in his hand as Homolka performed fellatio. In between, she would stop and talk:

(Video recording starts.)
HOMOLKA: I loved it when you fucked my little sister. I loved it when you fucked Tammy. I loved it when you took her

BERNARDO: Why?

HOMOLKA: Because it will make you happy.

BERNARDO: But why thirteen?

HOMOLKA: That's a good age.

BERNARDO: Because why?

HOMOLKA: Because they'll still be virgins.

BERNARDO: What are you saying?

(Homolka and Bernardo look at each other.)

HOMOLKA: I'm saying I think you should fuck them and take their virginity. Break their hymens with Snuffles. They're all our children, and I think you should make them ours even more.

BERNARDO: You're absolutely right. That's a good idea. When did you come up with it?

HOMOLKA: Just now.

(Homolka performs more oral sex on Bernardo and then gets up and walks out of camera range.)

HOMOLKA (off-camera): I have a surprise for you.

(Homolka re-enters camera range, and holding a paper bag in her hand, sits down beside Bernardo. From the bag she takes out a bra and panties and hands them to Bernardo.)

HOMOLKA: It's Tammy's.

(Bernardo smells Tammy's bra while

Homolka rubs his penis with the pantics.)
HOMOLKA: I want to rub Tammy's underwear all over your body. It will make you feel so good. I'm so glad you took her virginity, Paul. I wish we had four kids, Paul.

BERNARDO: Yes?

HOMOLKA: So you could fuck each one of them. (Rapidly rubbing the underwear on Bernardo's penis.) How does the king like that?

BERNARDO: Yeah.

HOMOLKA: I think the king should turn over.

BERNARDO: Okay.

HOMOLKA: Because his little slave has some more things to say and do. (Bernardo gets on his hands and knees while Homolka positions herself behind him. She probes his anus with one hand, licks it, while with the other hand she strokes his penis.)

BERNARDO: Oh, my little ass-licker. (After several minutes, they change positions. Bernardo lies on his back while Homolka strokes his penis with a long-stemmed rose.)

HOMOLKA: You know what we're going to do with this? (Holding up the rose to the camera.) We're going to take this to Tammy's tomorrow, and put it on her grave.

BERNARDO: Why?

HOMOLKA: Because it will give you pleasure. You loved her. She loved you. You were her favorite, you know. The things that you did, you know I loved it. The way you fucked her in what, sixty seconds? She loved it. She loved it.

BERNARDO: Your titties are bigger than hers.

HOMOLKA: I know.

BERNARDO: They taste better. When Tammy was alive, what did you used to do?

HOMOLKA: You made me lick it and suck it. And now I'm doing it on my own because I loved it, Paul. I loved everything you did with her. She was our little play toy. (Homolka resumes fellating Bernardo.)

BERNARDO: And we both loved her so much.

HOMOLKA: Yes, our little virgin. She loved us.

BERNARDO: What else?

HOMOLKA: I didn't give you my virginity, so I gave you Tammy's instead. I loved you enough to do that.

Homolka then began to talk about the girl Bernardo brought back to the house the night before.

HOMOLKA: (Clutching at Bernardo's penis.) You fucked her with this. You fucked her cunt. She sucked you. She

83

sucked Snuffles. She put it in her mouth, like this…You put her on her knees. You fucked her. And I let you do that because I love you, because you're the king…I want to do it again.

BERNARDO: When?

HOMOLKA: This summer, because the weather is too bad in the winter. If we can do that then it's good.

BERNARDO: Good.

HOMOLKA: If you want to do it fifty more times, we can do it fifty more times. If you want to do it every weekend, we can do it every weekend. Whenever we can. Because I love you. Because you're the king. Because you deserve it.

BERNARDO: Virgin cunts for me.

HOMOLKA: Yeah.

BERNARDO: Virgins just for me. It'll make me happy…going from one cunt to another, from one ass to another. Will you help me get the virgins?

HOMOLKA: Yes, I'll go in the car with you if you want, if you think that's best. Or I'll stay here and clean up afterward. I'll do everything I can because I want you to be happy. Because you're the king. (Homolka sucks on Bernardo's toes.)

BERNARDO: Oh, footsies.

HOMOLKA: Got to treat the king like a king.

BERNARDO: Good and what else?
HOMOLKA: I'm your little cocksucker. My nipples are so hard. I'm your cunt. Your little slut. Your little ass-licker. Your little virgin.
BERNARDO: (Raising his glass to the camera.) It's good to be king.
HOMOLKA: I'm your cunt-licking slut, the keeper of your virgins. Your ass-licking bitch. And I love you. I want to marry you.
(Video recording stops.)

The tape ended typically without Bernardo climaxing. It was an extraordinary insight into the minds and dynamics of a serial killer couple. Not only did they record their crimes, but also their intimate moments in which the fantasies of these crimes were brought to the surface.

Raping Jane Doe: "Why Couldn't It Have Been the Same with Tammy?"

Karla's parents were indeed tired of having Bernardo around. They were also upset by how Bernardo constantly hovered over their daughter, never leaving her alone with them. When they would speak with her, Bernardo would speak in her place. They asked Bernardo to move out, explaining that they needed privacy to grieve over Tammy's death. To their dismay, Karla moved out with Bernardo in a huff. The couple rented the house in the picturesque little lakeside town of Port Dalhousie, just outside of St. Catharines. Bernardo and Homolka were alone with their fantasies in their own private space.

Once alone with him, life with Bernardo became a horror story. Any time Karla made a mistake, Bernardo would unwind full punches to her upper arms—places where the bruising could be covered with a long-sleeved blouse. Another punishment he inflicted he called the "terrorist attack." He would wait until Karla had fallen asleep and then he'd suddenly jump on her, entering her anally and pummeling her with his fists. Her nights became long, restless stretches of semi-sleep, hovering between the nightmares of her dream-state and those of her waking life. One night, Bernardo was tossing and turning. Finding the bed too small, he pushed Homolka out on the floor. From that

night on, he insisted that she always sleep on the floor like a dog while he occupied the entire bed.

Not once did Homolka contemplate not marrying her Prince Charming. The wedding planning continued in earnest. In the meantime, Paul prowled at night and in the early mornings, attacking women and brutally raping them. On Saturday morning April 6, 1991, he raped a young woman jogging in Port Dalhousie, minutes away from their Cape Cod-style home. The relatively rare highly sadistic 'scripting' of the rape was indistinguishable from that of the Scarborough rapes and should have been immediately linked. But again, in those days, there was no system through which police in different jurisdictions could routinely compare details of similar crimes. It would have taken a special request, had police in Toronto even been aware of a rape taking place in Port Dalhousie.

On June 6, 1991, while Bernardo was out, Karla invited a 15-year-old girl known only as "Jane Doe" for a sleepover at their house. Karla had originally met the girl when the victim was twelve years-old; she used to hang around the pet-food store Karla worked in. Jane looked up to Karla and thought of her as a beautiful princess. She was a little surprised at the invitation but eagerly went over to the house in Port Dalhousie. As they watched the movie *Ghost*, Karla plied the girl with drinks spiked with sedatives. When the girl lost consciousness, Karla phoned Bernardo on his cell

phone, telling him to come home because she had a "surprise" wedding gift for him. When Paul got home, Karla offered up the unconscious girl to him.

Karla on the night she and Paul raped Jane Doe

Bernardo was unsure at first, expressing concern over what had happened to Tammy. Karla reassured Bernardo that this time she had the drug dosage under control. They videotaped themselves raping the unconscious girl. In the fifteen-minute videotape, Bernardo is seen forcing himself through the virgin girl's intact hymen, commenting, "Shit, I'll have to bust it." Karla rubbed her own genitals against Jane's face, rotating her hips lasciviously,

and then inserted the girl's limp fingers into her vagina while aping for the camera. Karla pretended to put a big, sloppy, fat kiss on the camera lens and performed cunnilingus on the girl.

The next day, Jane Doe awoke feeling sick but unaware of what had happened to her the night before. After driving the girl home that morning, Paul brutally punched Karla in the arm as he had a tendency to do when she did something he did not like. "What was that for?" Karla whined. "Everything went so smoothly with Jane," Paul complained. "Why couldn't it have been the same with Tammy?" But Karla had shown Paul she was ready to play and could even take the lead.

The Murder of Leslie Mahaffy

A week later, on the night of June 14-15, 1991—exactly two weeks before Bernardo and Homolka were to be married—Paul went out prowling as he often obsessively did. Bernardo had told Homolka that if he saw an appropriate "virgin" victim, he would kidnap her and bring her back. It did not seem to particularly concern Karla. That night, however, Bernardo had another mission in mind as he prowled the quiet residential suburbs of Burlington, yet another anonymous and affluent town in the Golden Horseshoe between Toronto and Niagara Falls. He had left his accounting job and was now a full-time liquor and cigarette smuggler. He used stolen license plates on his car during his smuggling runs in the belief that Canadian customs agents were staking out the parking lots of duty-free stores on the U.S. side and radioing back the license numbers of Canadian cars parked there.

Wearing a dark, hooded sweatshirt, Bernardo surreptitiously made his way between the dark yards and driveways of the sleeping housing tracts, looking for suitable license plates to steal. His prowling must have stirred all sorts of sexual associations for him of window peeping and pouncing on unsuspecting women to rape them. At about 2:30 a.m., Bernardo slipped into the backyard of Deborah and Dan Mahaffy's house. There he saw their 14-year-old daughter, Leslie, sitting alone in the dark of their backyard on a picnic bench.

Leslie Mahaffy was a cute girl with long, straight, honey blonde hair and braces gracing a warm smile. She was a highly spirited, independent,

and rebellious girl—but reasonably responsible. After one argument too many with her parents, she had recently run away from home. Unlike most teenage runaways, she did not run to the streets, but instead to the home of her best friend. Her friend's mother allowed her to stay there and Leslie phoned home every day, assuring her parents she was fine. After about ten days, tired of her independence, Leslie returned home; there seemed to be less tension with her parents.

The main issue had been that Leslie was expected to come home by 11:00 p.m. sharp. On Tuesday night, four of Leslie's fellow high school

friends were killed in a horrific car accident. That Friday, she and her friends had gathered together at the funeral home and later at a park to mourn their friends. Leslie's mother had dropped her off at the funeral home and told her that she could stay out a little later than 11:00 that night, but she was to phone home. Leslie stayed out until 1:30 a.m., and in a world before everybody had a cell phone, she never got a chance to get to a phone to call home.

A male friend of Leslie's walked her home. When they arrived at her house, everybody had gone to sleep. Her friend wanted to wait until she went inside, but Leslie assured him that she would go in through the side door, which was always left unlocked. Or so she thought. She told him to go home. Alone now, she discovered that both the side and back doors were locked. Leslie used to have a key, but when she ran away, her parents had changed the locks on the doors for some inexplicable reason. When Leslie returned home, they had not given her a copy of a new key. It was an act that cost their daughter her life.

Afraid that her mother would not let her go to the funeral the next day because of how late she was getting home, Leslie decided not to wake her parents up. At 2:00 a.m., using a public phone near her house, Leslie phoned her friend at whose house she had previously stayed. She wanted to go over and stay the night there, but her friend's mother would have to get up and drive over to pick Leslie up. That was not a good idea, the two girls agreed.

At about 2:20 a.m. Leslie hung up the phone and walked back to her house.

Leslie sat down on the family's picnic bench in their backyard and must have been wondering what to do next when Bernardo emerged out of the shadows. Standing before her was a handsome, blond, young man with an angelic face. Leslie asked, "What are you doing here?" Bernardo told her that he was burglarizing houses in the neighborhood.[5]

The rebellious 14-year-old's response was, "Cool." They chatted for a while and Leslie explained to Bernardo that she was locked out of her house. She then asked Bernardo for a cigarette. Paul replied that he had some in his car, which was parked on the next street. They walked through the warm June night over to his vehicle. Bernardo invited her to sit down inside his car. She agreed, but cautiously told him that she would keep the door open. She sat in the passenger seat with her legs dangling out on the road, smoking the cigarette that Bernardo had given her. He sat in the driver's seat. At one point, Leslie turned toward the open door to blow some smoke out. At that instant Bernardo pounced like an uncoiling snake: He leaned over and placed a knife around her throat and ordered her to lift her legs into the car. Bernardo then pushed her into the rear seat, blindfolded her, and threw a blanket over her. He then calmly drove thirty-five miles back to his home

at Port Dalhousie, assuring Leslie that if she did everything he told her, no harm would come to her.

As soon as Bernardo got Leslie into his house, he set up his video camera and began taping his assault of the girl. As the video camera rolled, Leslie was punched, slapped, her nipples were twisted by Bernardo, she was forced to urinate before the camera, to perform fellatio (with warnings from Bernardo not to scratch him with her braces), and was repeatedly raped and sodomized. She was kept blindfolded all the time. Fearing that she would be killed if she got another look at her assailants, every time the blindfold came loose, Leslie would alert Bernardo. She is seen in the video begging Bernardo not to kill her and crying that she desperately wants to see her baby brother again.

During this time Karla took their dog Buddy out for walks or sat downstairs reading the Bret Easton Ellis novel, *American Psycho*. Occasionally, when called, she would go upstairs and hold the video camera while Bernardo repeatedly raped the girl. When asked in court during her cross-examination how she could possibly walk the dog or read while a girl was being tortured and raped upstairs in her home, Karla missed the point of the question and incredulously replied that she was easily "capable of doing two things at once."

Karla was angry, but not because her husband was raping a teenage captive in their

house. She would later say to police, "Oh, I was really mad too because when I took Buddy out, there were two champagne glasses on the table, and we had these really expensive champagne glasses from France which we never used. He had those out. The two of them had been drinking champagne from those glasses. I was really mad."

Karla with their dog Buddy

It would be pointless and cruel to dwell here in these pages on the detailed transcripts of the torture and rape inflicted on Leslie Mahaffy. From the other video transcripts already quoted here, one can easily imagine what Karla and Bernardo put the girl

through and what was said. If any reader should need the exact details of what was on the videotapes of Leslie Mahaffy's rape and torture, they can refer to Toronto crime reporter Nick Pron's book, *Lethal Marriage*. Pron made the difficult decision to publish the transcripts in their entirety, and one such source should be enough.

Leslie Mahaffy suffered for nearly twenty-four hours. Sometime in the middle of the night, while Leslie lay handcuffed in the bedroom upstairs, Bernardo and Homolka went down to the kitchen and had a conference. There was a problem: It was Father's Day and Karla's parents were expected for dinner later in the day, their first visit to the house Karla and Paul had recently rented.

According to Karla, Bernardo decided that he had to kill Leslie because she would identify him if he let her go. Homolka says that she insisted on going upstairs and feeding Leslie sleeping pills so she would not feel anything when she died. Karla gave Leslie a teddy bear named Bunky that Bernardo had given her, to comfort the girl as she curled up in a fetal position and went to sleep. Then, Homolka says, Bernardo entered the room with a black electric cord, wrapped it around Leslie's throat, and attempted to strangle her. It was not easy. After the first attempt, Leslie gasped for life. Bernardo redoubled his effort until a pool of urine formed under Leslie as she died on the carpeted floor of their bedroom. Bernardo ordered Homolka to destroy the pillowcases and blanket stained with

Leslie's blood. Homolka argued that they were her favorite set of bedding. She would carefully wash them instead.

Bernardo took Leslie's body down to the basement and hid it in a cool corner. Then the couple went to bed to sleep as Leslie's urine dried on their floor. Bernardo let Karla sleep in the bed that night. They got up toward noon and Karla bustled about preparing dinner for her parents. When the Homolkas arrived, Bernardo took them for a tour of the house, carefully avoiding the basement where Leslie's body still lay.

On Monday morning, while Homolka went back to work at the clinic, Bernardo set up a clear plastic sheet in the form of a tent in the basement. He lined the bottom of it with sheets of newspaper. He then dragged Leslie's body into the tent and carved it into ten pieces with a circular power saw. The entire interior of the tent was splattered from top to bottom with blood, tissue, and body fluid which spilled out from the corpse. The electric saw was caked in flesh and bone. Bernardo attempted to wash it clean in the sink, but only succeeded in clogging up the drain with fatty body matter. Bernardo then went out and bought some quick-dry cement. Returning home, he encased the ten body parts into blocks of cement, and then stacked them in the basement.

Leaving the bloodied tent still standing, Bernardo went to the animal clinic and picked up Karla. He took her down to the basement and had

her put away the tent and clean out the body tissue and hair from the drain. Homolka testified that she used lemon-scented Lysol cleaner to clean up the basement. The couple then went upstairs and had dinner. Bernardo asked Homolka not to serve any meat for a while but laughed and joked how "light" Leslie's head was when he had cut it off.

The next evening, when Bernardo picked up Homolka from work, he told her that the concrete blocks were in the trunk of the car. The couple drove out to Lake Gibson, where they used to have sex when they were first dating, and threw the blocks into the water.

Police photo of Leslie Mahaffey's dismembered body part encased in concrete.

The remainder of the two weeks was busy for Homolka as she prepared the last details of her wedding. When she was being fitted for her

wedding dress, several of her friends noticed the bruises on her arms, but Homolka explained that she got them from handling dogs at the clinic.

On Saturday, June 29, 1991, the lavish wedding took place at the exclusive tourist town of Niagara-on-the-Lake. While Niagara Falls is a trashy and carnival-like town, full of cheap motels, casinos, and souvenir stands on the site of the famous waterfalls, Niagara-on-the-Lake, twenty minutes away, is an upscale elegant, Loyalist colonial settlement with an important theater center. At about the same time that Bernardo and Homolka were getting married, a fisherman was pulling out of Lake Gibson one of the concrete blocks Bernardo and Homolka had tossed in—the one they had not tossed far enough away from shore. That night, unaware that the police were piecing together Leslie Mahaffy's body, Bernardo and Homolka counted the money they had collected during the wedding. They had nine thousand dollars to spend on their honeymoon in Hawaii.

Karla would later complain in a police interview that Bernardo "ruined" her wedding night by confessing to her he was the infamous Scarborough Rapist. It was not the kind of wedding night a girl dreams of, she whined in the police videotape. Bernardo might have chosen the wedding night to confess in the mistaken belief that now married, his wife could not testify against him.

The Murder of Kristen French

After the murder of Leslie Mahaffy, Bernardo spent the next ten months routinely beating Homolka and stalking and raping other victims. On the Thursday afternoon before the Easter weekend of April 1992, Bernardo decided he needed another "virgin." He told Homolka to put her hair into a nonthreatening ponytail and the two drove over to the Holy Cross Catholic high school, near where Terri Anderson disappeared. Bernardo had already staked out the school. He was aroused by the school uniforms the girls wore: short plaid skirt, white blouse, and knee socks—a fairly common theme in erotic and pornographic media.

As students poured out of the school, Bernardo scanned the girls looking for one that suited his desire. He picked out 15-year-old Kristen French, a serious and studious young woman in grade 12. Bernardo followed her in his car. When he saw that she was walking alone, he passed her and pulled into a church parking lot just ahead. As Kristen came up toward the car, Karla called her over asking for directions. Standing in the open door of the auto, Karla had spread a map on the car's roof and asked Kristen to show her where they were. Kristen felt no fear in approaching the handsome young couple. As she began to scan the map, Bernardo circled behind her and pushed her into the vehicle. While Homolka held Kristen down in the backseat, Bernardo drove their captive to their home. For the next three days as Bernardo and Homolka both sexually assaulted Kristen, they videotaped everything. During the nights, they kept her drugged on sleeping pills, restrained and locked in the closet.

In the video, Bernardo urinated on and attempted to defecate on Kristen and had her chant, "I'm your 15-year-old Holy Cross sex slave," and "You're the most powerful man in the world. You deserve anything you want...You're so nice, powerful, sexy. So much in control of everything. Nobody can overpower you. Nobody...you're the king. The master. The king of all kings. The best man in the whole world. It's good that I'm getting punished."

Bernardo had Karla put on Tammy's similar schoolgirl uniform–type outfit and climb into bed with Kristen. He then ordered them to perform oral sex and masturbate each other. Bernardo barked out commands from behind the camera like a psycho film director: "Start licking at the bottom and work your way up to the top…Come on, let's hear some love stuff."

Karla told police in her interview: "So we dressed in almost identical uniforms and we put on makeup and we were giggling and laughing and it seemed like we're just friends getting ready to go out, kind of thing, we were doing what Paul had told us to do. I had all little perfume samples and she wanted to try some."

One is immediately incredulous—the raped and beaten, captive victim wanted to try perfume samples! Ridiculous!

But there it was in the videotapes, which surfaced later. As Homolka and Kristen stood in front of the bathroom mirror with cosmetics lined up on the counter, Bernardo switched on his video camera.

(Video recording starts.)
HOMOLKA: So what kind of perfume do you like?
KRISTEN: Eternity or Giorgio.
HOMOLKA: Yeah, I like Giorgio as well. I have some of that new perfume, Halston. I haven't worn it yet, but maybe I will today.

BERNARDO: Okay, girls, you know what I want you to do. Each one of you pull up your skirts at the same time. Okay, now bend over. Give me a nice ass shot. (Kristen does what she is told.)

BERNARDO: Good girls. Okay back to work.

HOMOLKA: Let's see what we have here.

KRISTEN: Eternity.

HOMOLKA: Oh, Eternity. I like it. That's Escape. I hate that one.

KRISTEN: Really? Can I smell it?

HOMOLKA: It's gross.

KRISTEN: I've never used it.

HOMOLKA: I was at work one day, and I bought one of those magazines, like Mademoiselle, and then the whole place stunk because of that perfume in a page. I've got others here to try, like Alfred Sung.

KRISTEN: Can I try this one?

HOMOLKA: Sure.

In explaining the scenes recorded on the videotape, Homolka recounted in court how Bernardo held a contest between her and Kristen. They were instructed to select and put on makeup and perfumes. Bernardo she said, told them, "The one who smells the best is the winner and won't get fucked by me up the ass."

BERNARDO: Tell the camera. Mmm, gorgeous, gorgeous.

(Bernardo leans forward and smells Kristen. He then smells Homolka.)

BERNARDO: No way, lady. This is not a nice smell.

HOMOLKA: (Sniffing Kristen's neck.) That is a nice smell.

BERNARDO: (To Kristen.) Even though you smell the best, I'm still going to fuck you up the ass anyways. She's my wife, after all. And she's got brownie points on her side.

The videotape revealed some surreal episodes in Kristen French's three-day ordeal at the hands of Bernardo and Homolka. There were moments when one would not guess that Kristen was a captive in the hands of homicidal monsters who were raping her and were about to murder her. Some of these horrific episodes are reproduced here because they illuminate the subtle dynamics between a victim and her killers—the razor's edge between life and death at the hands of a serial killer.

In the midst of her nightmarish ordeal, Kristen French appears to cleverly and desperately attempt to survive and manipulate her captors. In one video segment, Kristen and Karla are videotaped by Bernardo having sex with each other:

HOMOLKA: I like you, Kristen.

KRISTEN: I like you, too.

HOMOLKA: Do you want to have some fun?

KRISTEN: Sure, okay. How come your teeth are so straight?

HOMOLKA: I don't know. How about yours?

KRISTEN: (giggling) You're silly.

HOMOLKA: (Undressing Kristen.) Don't be so nervous. It's okay.

KRISTEN: Am I shaking?

HOMOLKA: No. Just try to feel at home. You have nice legs.

KRISTEN: This one's kind of short.

HOMOLKA: That's okay.

KRISTEN: Can I ask you a favor? Before I leave, can I see your dog...without it attacking me?

(Homolka looks up toward Bernardo behind the camera.)

HOMOLKA: It's up to him.

BERNARDO: Yeah, sure. Before you leave.

KRISTEN: I like dogs.

BERNARDO: Me, too.

Some interpreted Kristen French's easygoing banter with Homolka and Bernardo as symptoms of her succumbing to Stockholm syndrome—where shocked and disorientated captives begin to relate to and associate themselves with their captors. In Kristen's case, it is unlikely. It is clear from

Kristen's dialogue that she had her wits about her and was cleverly attempting to create a context in her relationship with her captors in which her release would be inevitable. Kristen positively said, "*Before I leave*, can I see your dog?" It was a courageous and intelligent attempt at survival and one that could have potentially worked had she been in the hands of serial killers with a slightly different profile. Bernardo does not miss Kristen's futile attempt though, when he responds, "Yeah, sure. *Before you leave*." He is on to her. It's heart-breaking. We know as the videotape rolls forward they are going to kill her.

While Kristen was held captive, Bernardo left the house on two occasions to get takeout food, leaving her alone with Homolka. The moment Bernardo was out the door, Kristen desperately pleaded with Karla to let her escape, but Karla refused.

"What Do You Know About Dying?"

On the third day of her captivity, Kristen French began to openly resist Bernardo, refusing to obey his commands—not the behavioral path a Stockholm syndrome victim takes. Bernardo then showed her the videotape of Leslie Mahaffy being raped and tortured, saying to Kristen, "You know who that is, don't you? What happened to her will happen to you if you don't do what I tell you."

Kristen must have been horrified to recognize the face of the girl who had been reported missing and had been found dismembered at Lake Gibson. Despite the horror, the courageous 15-year-old Kristen French refused to comply further with Bernardo's perverted demands and defiantly countered, "There are some things worth dying for." Bernardo responded with a sustained cycle of vicious punches and kicks to her body.

Homolka and Bernardo raped her again several more times before Bernardo commenced beating her yet again. One of the last images on the video was of Kristen lying tied up and battered almost into unconsciousness. On the video, she spits out at Bernardo: "I don't know how your wife can stand being around you."

"Just shut up, okay. Just shut up," Bernardo is heard saying on the video, just before turning the camera off.

Shortly afterward, Bernardo took an electrical cord and wrapped it around Kristen's

throat. He carefully timed himself for seven minutes as he held his grip. Karla stated she heard Bernardo mutter in Kristen's ear as he killed her: "What do you know about dying?"

If in Dante's *Inferno* there was a "He-Said-She-Said Psycho Newlyweds Game Show," then Bernardo and Homolka would have been star contestants. While Homolka testified that Bernardo killed the girls, Bernardo stated that Homolka killed both of the girls when he left them alone with her. Bernardo said he wanted to keep Kristen French as a sex slave and not kill her. Homolka became jealous, he asserts, and killed Kristen. This is conceivable, for along with *American Psycho*, the other book that Bernardo had on hand at the time was *Perfect Victim*, by Christine McGuire and Carla Norton. The book was a true-crime account of a 20-year-old woman who was kidnapped in California and kept as a sex slave for seven years by a married couple. Furthermore, the autopsy report on Leslie Mahaffy showed bruising on her back consistent with a pair of knees pressed there the size and shape of Karla's. It should also be noted that the only time Bernardo's many female victims died, was when Karla was present. Alone, Bernardo had not killed any of his rape victims.

Karla insisted that Bernardo had killed Kristen because the couple was due at her parents' house for Easter dinner. She stated that Bernardo then forced her to clean up the evidence. Because there might be carpet fibers in Kristen's hair from

Bernardo's rug, rather than destroying her precious rug, Karla stupidly hacked off Kristen's hair and collected it in a bag.

She and Bernardo then carried her body into the bathroom and submerged it in the tub. Her corpse was scrubbed clean, because Bernardo told Karla that the police were able to lift fingerprints from flesh. He ordered Karla to douche Kristen's vagina and anus clean of Bernardo's seminal fluids. Bernardo burned her clothes, hair, and the sports bag she was carrying when she was taken captive, in the fireplace downstairs and then carefully collected the ashes for disposal. He meticulously wiped clean the glass face of Kristen's watch, and then shattered it.

To make it seem like the killers lived in Burlington, where Mahaffy had been kidnapped, Homolka and Bernardo planned to dump Kristen's body on Leslie Mahaffy's grave, but they couldn't find it. In the end, they tossed Kristen out by the side of the road leading to the cemetery. She was found naked and shorn of her hair fourteen days after she had gone missing.

"It didn't sound logical that he would be out abducting her and cutting her up and then getting married..."

By now the multi-million dollar Green Ribbon Taskforce (GRT) had been formed in the Niagara Region to look into several disappearances and murders of young women including Leslie Mahaffey and Kristen French. When witnesses reported sighting an older model unkempt Camaro in the vicinity of Kristen French's abduction, billboards with the sinister-looking car went up all over the province.

Bernardo did not escape police attention as a suspect in the murders. Again, it was Bernardo's acquaintances, Alex and Tina Smirnis, who had first gone to police in September 1990 about the Scarborough rapes, who through a personal acquaintance in the Ontario Provincial Police brought Bernardo up as a suspect in May 1992. The tip came in like this in a police report:

> PC Haney received info from anonymous party re Paul K. Bernardo 27 Aug. 64 from 57 Bayview Dr. [Port Dalhousie] St. Catharines. Mr. Bernardo was a suspect in the Scarborough rape cases & lived in Scarborough. He has been seen hitting women & raped a girl in his basement while his wife was upstairs. He has a Nissan

240SX, yellow, 660HFH. He is attracted to small women with short hair. He attended Scarborough College. Male is very violent and hostile–short hair–shaves hair on back of head–wavy and curly on top–appears intelligent and perceptive–admits to beating wife–has hit girls on three occasions. Went to Scarboro College. Has been questioned by Metro for Scarboro Rapist. Aggressive toward women. Raped a girl in basement of house. Can only grow hair on chin. 21 Sir Raymond Richmond 2 years ago moved to St. Cth. likes small petite women, short hair Scar. Rapist susp. clothing good tan. had been in Florida and had tan. Once rape takes place he disassociate with friends and family for a few weeks. Drives 89 Nissan 240.Yellow. 660HFH

On May 12, 1992, two detectives appeared at the Bernardos' house, the very house in which the two girls had been raped and murdered. Again, as in every previous instance, a criminal background check on Bernardo came back showing no prior charges. The police officers filed the following report.

On 92.05.12 investigating officers attended at 57 Bayview Dr., and interviewed PAUL BERNARDO, dob 64.08.27. Paul BERNARDO had been called in as a

possible suspect by P.C. Rob HANEY, BEAVERTON O.P.P. (705) 426 7366.

Paul BERNARDO had been questioned during the investigation of the Scarborough Rapist.

Paul BERNARDO resides at 57 Bayview Dr., with his wife KARLA (maiden name HOMOLKA). They were married on June 29, 1991. Karla works at the Martindale Animal Clinic as an Animal Health Technician. Paul is an Accountant but presently unemployed. When questioned about his whereabouts on April 16th, he stated he would most likely have been home as he is writing the lyrics for a song.

Paul BERNARDO does not own a Camaro. The only vehicle registered to the BERNARDO'S is a 1989 Nissan 240 licence 660 HFH (Ont) 2 dr. yellow.

Paul BERNARDO advised he was called in on the Scarborough Rapist investigation and asked to supply hair samples, to which he complied. He appeared slightly nervous while being interviewed but was willing to answer all questions.

Detective Nesbitt who had conducted the interview would later state:

> We had the information he had been called in to Metro on the Scarborough Rapist. What threw me off, when I asked him "have

you ever been in trouble?" he said immediately "no I haven't but I was called in on the Scarborough Rapist investigation and gave samples" and they showed him the composite and he said "I have to be honest I do look like the composite." He was quite open and honest about it. We went through his history of when he got married... Knowing when Leslie was abducted and the week previous he was getting married. It didn't sound logical that he would be out abducting her and cutting her up and then getting married. He was well groomed and it was a well-kept house... I looked at the car and here you got a new model Nissan. I am under the impression we were looking for an older car. My partner had a Camaro and we agreed it didn't look like a Camaro. It was a month after the abduction and you are asking what you are doing on April 16th. He couldn't recall but he believed he was home...His wife was working and he picked her up... I called Metro the next day because after his interview we interviewed a couple of other people... He appeared slightly nervous. That was normal because it was such a serious offense. That didn't put in a lot of weight. Most were nervous.

When the whole case was over and done with several years later, and government review of its failures would report:

> When putting Nesbitt's interview with Bernardo in context, it should be noted that it is common in serial predator investigators for the police to interview the killer several times without connecting him to the deaths. Predatory psychopathic killers can be very plausible and appear very innocent. They do not typically reveal themselves during police interviews. It is a commonplace of such investigations that the Yorkshire Ripper was interviewed by the police at least 9 times during the course of his six-year series of 7 attacks and 13 murders. The GRT investigators were keenly aware of that spectre. As one of them said:

> > We were all told and lived with the fear that we would interview the culprit and not know. We all lived with that fear.

> This fact was stressed to the investigators by Inspector Bevan:

> > We used the Bundy thing over and over again. How he was interviewed several times before someone caught on, and how when you are dealing with a psychopath, it is not only in

their nature, it's their practice to win interview situations like this, so you don't go in there expecting to find someone with it stamped on their forehead....because they're probably going to be very congenial with you and look totally normal and the whole situation is going to look normal to you... Nobody wanted to be the person who spoke to this guy and missed him... I'm not attaching any kind of blame or onus on the people who spoke to him and didn't pick up on the fact that he was the one because he was pretty good.[6]

The shocking truth of the matter is, that in unsolved serial killer cases, the perpetrator's identity is often already somewhere in the police paperwork, sometimes even among lists and interview reports on people police have already identified as possible suspects, met, and interviewed, not just once, but multiples of times.

"Leslie's coming for you! She's down there in the basement. Right where I cut her up."

As soon as police left, Bernardo and Karla now hid the videotapes and Paul's favorite knife in the insulation of the rafter in their garage. Karla would later testify that Paul told her to destroy the tapes if police came back or if he was arrested.

Bernardo and Homolka went on for another eight months. There were more beatings for Karla, Bernardo was out stalking and raping women, Homolka and he engaged prostitutes for three-way sex. Bernardo was drinking heavily and beating Karla almost daily, and was now striking her in the face and pulling out clumps of her hair. Once Bernardo threw her down into the cold cellar, turned off the light, and bolted the door, screaming down to his terrified wife, the horror movie fan, "Leslie's coming for you! She's down there in the basement. Right where I cut her up." Karla spent the night locked in the dark cellar with her ghosts.

Bernardo drove around with Karla in the car, pointing out women he was stalking and telling her he was going to rape them next. Once, while watching a woman on the street, he masturbated, making Karla look the other way. At other times, he had Karla perform fellatio on him as he watched his potential victims. She stupidly stood by her man as he disintegrated.

"Raccoon Face"

Bernardo owned a Maglite—a long-handled flashlight manufactured out of gun barrel–hard anodized 6061 aluminum. The flashlights are carried by police officers because of their durability and usefulness as a baton. There are several cases of individuals being killed from blows of a Maglite wielded by a police officer. When Bernardo began to beat Karla in the face with the flashlight on December 27, 1992, now in fear of her life, she finally ran. Before escaping with her eyes almost swollen shut black and blue, she attempted to retrieve the videotapes that they hid in the garage, but by then Bernardo, suspicious of Karla, had moved them. Badly bruised and swollen, Karla showed up at her parents' house on January 5, 1993. They immediately took her to an emergency ward and Bernardo was charged with domestic assault that night.

In order that Bernardo could not find her, the Homolkas sent her to Toronto to stay with her aunt and uncle, Patricia and Calvin Seger. The tenants in the Segers' apartment building nicknamed the mysterious blonde with the bruises under her eyes "Raccoon Face." Within weeks, however, Homolka was out partying at a disco and quickly found herself a new lover. She told him nothing about her past other than that she was going through a "bad divorce."

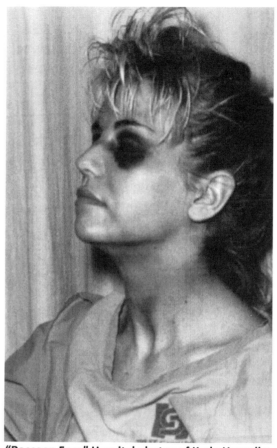

"Raccoon Face" Hospital photos of Karla Homolka

In the meantime, Bernardo was rambling around the empty house, shouting for Karla. "Snuggle Bunny, are you home, Karly Curls?" He recorded a videotape directed to Karla in which he threatened suicide: "I need you, Kar. I love you, my princess, my queen, my everything. I think about you every

day now…I realize now you're never coming back. Fucking kills me, pal. I wish I just could have been given a second chance to make things right…I know you had to leave, and I don't blame you. In fact, it was the best thing you could have done for me. It snapped me out of whatever state I was in. It made me realize how much I care for you…You are the most special person who ever touched my life. Yes, even more than Tammy. When you know you've lost it all, and there's no one to turn to, death's welcome mat is the only place you can go… Okay, I fucked up this life, right? When I go to the other side, okay, I'm going to make it better for you there. I'm going to set something up real nice. So when you come, it'll be all right. You know what I'm saying?"

Busted

When it ended, it ended fast but dirty. On February 1, 1993, three weeks after Karla left Bernardo, like a time bomb with a twenty-six month fuse the Bernardo's DNA sample finally came back from the Centre of Forensic Studies to the police. In the wake of start-up pains, Ontario government-funding cutbacks, and bureaucratic mismanagement, it had taken twenty-six months to run the tests which, had they been made a priority, could have been done in a month. Paul Bernardo, the polite young accountant, was their man.

The police immediately deployed a twenty-four-hour surveillance around Bernardo. They followed him as he stalked women in his car. Police began to focus in on him as a prime suspect in the Leslie Mahaffy and Kristen French murders. On February 9, police visited Karla Homolka at the Segers' home   They pointedly asked her if she had ever cut anyone's hair and whether she had been in the church parking lot from which French was kidnapped (without telling Homolka why they were asking). Homolka was in a state of panic. After the police left, Homolka told her aunt and uncle that Bernardo had videotaped her and Bernardo having sex with Leslie Mahaffy and Kristen French, and that Homolka had looked for the tapes before she left. The Segers immediately took her to see a lawyer, George Walker, who now began to shelter Karla as a client.

On February 14, Walker confirmed for police and prosecution that Bernardo was not only a rapist but a murderer and that some of the sexual assaults on Mahaffy and French had been recorded on videotape and that Homolka had looked for them unsuccessfully before she had fled 57 Bayview Drive. She thought that they were kept in the same hiding place as the knife Bernardo used to intimidate his victims, and she thought that the knife was in its hiding place but not the tapes.

On February 17, 1993, Bernardo was arrested and charged with the Scarborough rapes.

As Bernardo was pulled out of the house and taken away to jail, the police immediately began an intense forensic search of the house on 57 Bayview. Wearing spaceman-like suits so that they did not contaminate the site, the police forensic technicians tore out the walls, they drilled holes in the floor, they wrenched out the plumbing, they ripped out the carpeting, pried loose the baseboards, vacuumed up every loose hair and piece of lint, and dusted every square inch for fingerprints. The police technicians spent seventy-one days inside the Port Dalhousie death house, and despite knowing that there were videotapes of the assaults on Mahaffey and French, except for an edited 1:58 minute video showing a comatose teenage girl being sexually abused by both Bernardo and Homolka, police could not find any other video evidence linking Bernardo to the two murdered girls.

At first police thought the unconscious victim in the 1:58 video clip might have been Kristen French, but the teenage victim would be later found alive and identified only as "Jane Doe". By identifying a rental movie VHS video case visible in the background of the occurring rape and checking local video store rental records for the title, police determined the date of attack as being the night of June 6-7, 1991, shortly before the couple's wedding day. But experienced police evidence technicians completely failed to find a key piece of evidence secreted by Bernardo in the house in a hiding place as moronically simple as one used by kids to hide their stash.

"The 'cycle of abuse'... She was a naive, simple, innocent helpless child..."

Karla Homolka, in the meantime, had been told by everybody—doctors, police, nurses, social workers, family, and friends, all unaware of her role in the crimes—that obviously she was a battered wife. She was a victim here. Soon Homolka began to believe it herself and, smart as a whip, she read up on battered spouse syndrome and post-traumatic stress disorder, mastering the jargon and its symptoms. In describing her relationship with Bernardo, Karla frequently used the terms "cycle of abuse" and "learned helplessness," terms set out in Lenore Walker's definitive 1979 book, *The Battered Woman*.

On the advice of her attorney, George Walker, Karla was hospitalized on March 4, 1993 at Toronto's former Northwestern General Hospital for seven weeks of psychiatric observation and treatment for *dysthymia,* also known as "reactive depression," and severe post-traumatic stress disorder (PTSD), as defined in the American Psychiatric Association's Diagnostic Manual, *D.S.M. III-R.* Karla put on a good show for the psychiatrists at the hospital. Videotapes of Karla being interviewed by police show a very prim, well dressed, hair demurely tied back or falling gently around her small shoulders, intelligent, articulate young woman speaking calmly and evenly, but in a

thin, helpless little girl's voice. Karla looked small and gave off a vibe of feminine vulnerability that draws one into a protective urge; the cops and the doctors fell for it and ate up everything she dished out.

The head psychiatrist at Northwestern General, Dr. Hans J. Arndt, compared Karla to a concentration camp survivor. Dr. Andrew Malcolm, a staff psychiatrist with extensive forensic experience and a clinical psychologist concluded that Karla was an extreme case of "abused spouse syndrome" and was a classic victim of torture. The psychiatrist reported:

> In addition there are all of the factors that constitute psychological torture as defined by Amnesty International. There was social isolation, exhaustion stemming from deprivation of sleep, monopolization of perception through the exhibition of intensely possessive behaviour, threats of death against the person or the person's relatives, humiliation and denial of power, and the administration of drugs or alcohol to diminish self-control. Karla was systematically subjected to all of these things. Karla was subjected to repeated sadistic sexual attacks. She was humiliated, beaten, tied up and raped over a period of years. She was manipulated into being a participant in what eventuated in the death

of a much-loved sister. She was advised on her wedding night that her new husband was a rapist. She was told that if she ever tried to leave her husband he would track her down and kill her. Or else he would kill her remaining sister and her parents. She was living with a sexual sadist and she was convinced that from this bewildering fate there was no escape.

Years later when the case was over and Karla's participation in the rapes and murders revealed at the trial, Dr. Malcolm continued to defend Karla, insisting she was Bernardo's victim, "She was a naive, simple, innocent helpless child who was impressed by what her parents thought of her catch and what her little girlfriends thought of her catch. She was overwhelmed by this fellow."

Despite the fact that Karla was living at home with her family and Bernardo was visiting her only on weekends, Karla claimed she was helpless to resist Paul's demands to assist him in the Christmas drugging and rape of her little sister. When a journalist cornered Dr. Malcolm on this issue, asking him how Karla could have been under such control of Bernardo while still living at home when she offered up her little sister as a 'present' to Bernardo, the psychiatrist weakly responded, "She became dependent on him. He controlled her. He advised her she was worthless. I don't think she was a full-blown battered wife but I think the early

beginnings of it were already under way. She was already falling into his thrall at that point. That was my opinion when I saw her, that she was in fact an 'influenced' person."

Asked if she wasn't therefore a "battered spouse" at that point when she participated in the sexual assault on her little sister, what was she therefore suffering from? Dr. Malcolm could only concede, "I can't really answer that. I think it was an outrageous act."

Karla was actually becoming jealous and resentful of the attention that Bernardo was focusing on her little sister. She would later recollect how angry she was when, during a pool party at their house, Tammy and Paul snuck off by themselves and remained absent long after all the guests departed while Karla was left alone simmering in humiliation.

Karla played the role of traumatized victim with aplomb. Whenever police would come up with something Homolka had neglected to mention, like, for example, her luring and drugging on her own initiative of Jane Doe for Bernardo to rape, Homolka would claim 'post-traumatic stress–related memory loss' as a result of her victimization by Bernardo.

Police videotapes of Karla's interviews reveal the callous creature lurking beneath the figure of the demure petite blonde. For every day of taping, Karla would wear a different fashionable outfit. A police video camera accompanied Karla's

interview in the house of horror at 57 Bayview as she walked police through the various crime scenes. For this occasion, Karla chose to put her hair into a braid and wear a schoolgirl's outfit with a short plaid skirt, white hose and little girl school shoes, maybe even the very same "Tammy" outfit she wore for Bernardo. As they walked around the house, Karla asked the police if any of her furniture had been damaged in the police search.

Karla, dressed for the occasion in a schoolgirl outfit, tours police through the house demonstrating for their video camera how the victims were raped and tormented.

In the master bathroom upstairs where Karla was videotaped in the "perfume competition" with captive Kristen French and where Kristen's corpse was later bathed clean of forensic evidence, Karla is only concerned about what happened to all her

cosmetics and perfume samples. At one point when in the basement where Leslie Mahaffey was dismembered, she looks down at the rug and comments that her sister wants it. When the police officer replies that for the time being it has to remain as evidence, Karla complains, "I'll have to clean it."[7]

"We were in a situation we *needed* to do this."

When Karla Homolka's lawyer came forward with offer for her testimony against Bernardo in exchange for a lenient sentence, the prosecutors seemed interested because they had come up with very little evidence in the house linking Bernardo to the murder of Mahaffy and French, other than trace DNA samples to Mahaffy. It proved Mahaffy was in the house, but not that Bernardo necessarily had murdered her. Even though the prosecution had viewed the 1:58 sliced video showing Homolka gleefully assaulting "Jane Doe," they had only circumstantial evidence for murder charges. As Niagara Police Inspector Vince Bevan, the chief investigator in the case, will later explain about the deal, "Did we want to do this or did we *need* to do this? We were in a situation we *needed* to do this."

As these negotiations with Homolka were taking place, on April 29, 1993, the police search warrant on Bernardo's house expired. Police had been in the house for seventy-one days, had already renewed the warrant its maximum three times and were now required to vacate the house by May 1.

The owners who had rented the house to Paul and Karla were anxious to take the home back into their possession. But Paul Bernardo's lawyer, Ken Murray, continued paying rent on the house throughout the period of the police search, legally

retaining the house in Bernardo's possession as per the lease. Raping, murdering and dismembering victims in the house was not a breach of the written terms of the lease. Evicting Bernardo would become a drawn-out process if he decided to be uncooperative with the owners and file appeals. The owners were only happy to give Murray unsupervised access to the house to remove Paul Bernardo's remaining property that police had not seized for evidence in order that Bernardo would vacate the premises as soon as possible.

On May 6, a week after police had left, Ken Murray and his co-counsel, Carolyn MacDonald, along with office manager and law clerk Kim Doyle, entered the house and guided by Bernardo on a jailhouse phone to Murray's cell phone, the three "officers of the court" proceeded to the master bathroom upstairs. There Murray climbed up on the vanity and unscrewed a ceiling lamp, reached in with his arm under the roof insulation, and withdrew a stash of six small Hi-8 video cassettes: the rape and torture videos of Tammy Homolka, Leslie Mahaffey, Kristen French, and the original "Jane Doe" tape, that the police failed to find in their seventy-one day search of the small house. And then Murray did something that would outrage everybody and raise a howl for his head; he concealed from the police and the prosecution his possession of the tapes for the next seventeen months.[8]

Murray had recovered the tapes a week *before* the plea deal with Homolka had been signed and sealed by the prosecutors on May 14. Had Ken Murray, as defense attorneys in Canada (and perhaps the United States) are required to do when they come into *possession of physical evidence*, resigned as Bernardo's attorney and turned the tapes over to police immediately, the deal with Karla might not have been necessary. But Murray didn't and Karla's plea deal went through as he sat on the tapes.

In exchange for a guilty plea to manslaughter and her testimony against Bernardo on charges of murder, Homolka negotiated a maximum sentence of twelve years. With good behavior, Karla would be eligible for parole after serving four years, or without it, she was eligible for automatic statutory release after eight years under Canadian penal law, and four on parole. The prosecution agreed not to contest her parole application.

Obstruction of Justice

No wonder everybody wanted Ken Murray's head after it had been revealed he had been hiding the videotapes. The prosecution, police and the government loved it, because it allowed them to blame Murray for the controversial deal that they gave to Karla, despite the lack of investigative performance of the forensic techs who failed to find the hidden tapes during the prolonged search of the house.

In his defence, Murray stated that while Bernardo instructed him to recover the videotapes, he had also instructed Murray not to view them. Bernardo's exact written instructions were, "We will have to go through them in the future. At this time I instruct you not to view them." Murray said he did not know the tapes were evidence. It's only when Bernardo was charged with the murders on May 18 that Murray first viewed the tapes in his possession, but by then the Homolka deal had been sealed and delivered.

When Murray took the tapes on May 6, he did not know that Homolka was negotiating a deal. (Although it did not take a genius attorney to guess that Karla's lawyer would be trying to get her a deal.) Murray only learned that a deal had been made somewhere between May 14 and May 17, but he would not know some of details of the deal until six months later, and the full details until a full year later in May 1993.

The problem for Murray is that a defence attorney can conceal what a client *tells* them in privilege, but they may not conceal physical evidence. Normally in what is known as the "warm gun" principle, when a client approaches an attorney with incriminating evidence like a murder weapon, (a just-fired handgun, thus the "warm gun") the attorney warns the client off and does his best to weasel out of taking custody of that evidence or being "aware" of its existence. Otherwise the attorney now has become a material witness and must immediately resign from his client's defence and surrender the physical evidence to the prosecution.

Even defence attorneys are considered "officers of the court" and must act in the pursuit of justice, even while acting in defence of their client. An attorney must give his client the "best defence" but one that is "fair" to the pursuit of true justice that the attorney as an "officer of the court" must perform. To knowingly conceal physical evidence is a criminal offence known as "obstruction of justice."

Had Murray simply *heard* in confidence from Bernardo about the videotapes and their location and then *did nothing*, he might have been acting within attorney-client privilege. But Murray ended up taking the tapes into his custody, physically moving them, duplicating them and concealing them, which was grounds for obstruction of justice. (Damning Murray to a charge of

obstruction of justice later was his omission of video duplication costs on his Legal Aid billing because he feared it may tip off prosecution that he had the videotapes in his possession.)[9]

When the deal with Homolka was made, Murray now felt that he had in the videotapes something that would expose the prosecution's star witness Karla not as a victim, but for what she was, Bernardo's enthusiastic co-perpetrator in the rapes and murders of her sister Tammy, Leslie Mahaffy and Kristen French. This would discredit her as a witness against his client. He argued that since he had not been informed of the details of the Homolka deal or given discovery of her testimony, he strategically withheld the tapes to better mount a defence for his client, Bernardo.

Gradually, however, it began to dawn on Murray, that while the videotapes exposed Karla Homolka and discredited her, at the same time they also exposed and incriminated his client Bernardo in the charges he was facing. It also became clear to him just how immense of an error he might have made in concealing those tapes and the devastating impact this could have on his future career. In August 1994 Ken Murray resigned from the case, retained a lawyer for himself and turned the videotapes over to police on September 22, 1994, as he should have seventeen months earlier. Just in time for the upcoming trial but way too late to have any impact on Homolka's plea-bargain deal.

After Bernardo was convicted in September 1995 of all charges, in January1997 Murray was charged with obstructing justice, conspiracy to obstruct justice, possessing child pornography and making obscene materials when copying the tapes. The latter two charges were later dropped by the prosecution. Murray's co-counsel, Carolyn MacDonald, was also charged with obstructing justice and possession of child pornography, although all charges against MacDonald were dropped in May 1997.[10]

The entire Scarborough Rapist-Bernardo-Homolka investigation and prosecution had been such a cluster-fuck that it was evident that Murray was being conveniently scapegoated, as much as he played his role well in the cluster. Wisely Murray chose to be tried before a judge without a jury. On June 13, 2000, the judge acquitted Murray of the remaining criminal charge of obstruction of justice on the grounds that Murray did not sufficiently understand the contents and context of the videotapes to have knowingly perpetrated an obstruction of justice. In September 2000 all law society professional misconduct charges were dropped as well.

"I Hope They Let Me Do My Hair in Jail. I Would Just Die If My Hair Went to Hell."

The sensational trial of Paul Bernardo began in May 1995. The videotapes would become a focus of the trial as it dragged on in Toronto into the hot summer months. Two 30-inch video monitors on six-foot platforms draped in funerary black cloth faced the courtroom audience and press gallery. Another two monitors faced the jury while the legal teams, the judge and Bernardo had small monitors to view. A huge sound system boomed the videotape audio into the courtroom.

First the prosecution showed the porn video 'selfies' Paul and Karla made, close-ups of her masturbating with a wine bottle on 30-inch screens, performing lollypop blow-jobs and licking ass. It was quite the introduction to the prosecution's upcoming star witness. The lines trying to get a rare courtroom seat went around the block.

Then came the real sick horrific shit: the rape and torture videos of Tammy Homolka, Leslie Mahaffey and Kristen French. The audience monitors were switched off and the videos were shown in court only to the jury and court but away from the audience and press who could still hear the audio.

As Karla waited in her cell for the time when she would be called to testify in court, she

preened and primped with her hair, writing her friend Wendy, "am letting my bangs grow. I want to look my best when I go to court and see Paul. I want him to drool when he sees me." She testified against Bernardo in June, portraying herself as just one more of his victims. Her testimony on that account was hardly believable. The jury had watched the tapes and saw Karla willingly participating and enjoying the rapes and tortures of the victims. But there was nothing they could do. The deal was done. At issue was not her participation in the rapes, but Karla's testimony on Paul Bernardo's murders of the girls.

Paul Bernardo admitted to raping the girls. In view of the videotapes, he could take no other position. He denied, however, killing Mahaffy and French. He insisted that both girls died while in Karla's custody. Near the end of his testimony, Bernardo admitted that he had some "problems" with his sexuality. "Down the road, I'm going to have to seek professional help for it," Bernardo flatly stated, not understanding why a wave of scornful laughter rippled through the courtroom.

In the end, Bernardo was sentenced to life imprisonment in 1995 (Canada has no death penalty) without possibility of parole for twenty-five years. He was then declared as a Dangerous Offender which under Canadian law allows for "indefinite" incarceration of an offender deemed dangerous to release at the discretion of the Parole Board of Canada. It is unlikely that Paul Bernardo

will ever get out of prison alive. Until about 2012 Bernardo remained in isolated solitary confinement, in the protective segregation unit as a sex offender, a leading candidate in the prison system for shanking. The only relief for Bernardo were visits from police attempting to clear other cases of rapes and murderers that they thought Bernardo might have committed.

But in 2012, it was finally decided to risk Bernardo's life in the prison population. He was last reported to be working in the prison library. In 2014, to nobody's surprise, the press reported that Paul Bernardo might be marrying an admirer, a 30-

year-old woman from London, Ontario, convinced that Paul is innocent. Sporting a recent tattoo on her ankle in cursive letters, "Paul's Girl," the woman told the Toronto Sun, "He is a kind man, a Christian, a very nice man."[11]

Karla's prison record would be more controversial. The Mean Girl thrived in prison, taking college courses, engaging in lesbian love affairs and throwing prison block parties. She posed in photos tending flowers in the prison garden and among toys and props used in battered women therapy sessions. In chatty letters from prison to her friends, Homolka wrote on her arrival there: "There are some people, like you, who know that this horror is not of my own making." She wrote that prison was an opportunity for her to take some university courses: "I want you to know that life in here isn't as bad as most people think...Hopefully, I'll be able to finish my degree while I'm here. I'm eligible for parole in four years and intend to be out —for sure!"

Her only worry about prison: "I hope they let me do my hair in jail. I would just die if my hair went to hell."

Karla did not get out in four years, nor in eight. Public indignation over the deal and a constant barrage of media coverage of Karla's every prison block party, her lesbian relationships, her love affair through a fence with a male prisoner convicted of murdering his girlfriend, her prison psychiatric file, her university courses, her

Victoria's Secrets gifts, her hair, her personal letters and photographs, all that coverage and public outcry drove the correctional system to keep Karla in prison until she had served her full term of twelve years. It's all there on the internet in its every sensational detail.

Karla clowning in the prison "theater therapy" room. The sign she holds reads in French: "Do you miss me?"

Karla Unbound

Karla's prison sentence came to an end on American Independence Day on July 4, 2005, and her release the next day received frenzied helicopter-convoy media coverage. In an attempt to pre-empt the media from hounding her for an interview, she appeared two hours after her release on Canada's national broadcaster, the CBC, interviewed in French, because she claimed that the French-language Quebec media was the only one that treated her fairly. She was driven straight from the prison to the interview hidden in the backseat of her lawyer, Sylvie Bordelais's car.

Karla as she appeared in her CBC interview on the day of her release from prison. (Courtesy of Radio-Canada CBC)

In the nationally televised interview, Karla said, in a very fluent French, "I cry often. I can't

forgive myself. I think about what I did and often I think I don't deserve to be happy because of what I did. What I did was terrible and I was in a situation where I was unable to see clearly, where I was unable to ask for help, where I was completely overwhelmed in my life... Back then I was seventeen years old. I didn't know much. I was and I regret it enormously because now I know I had the power to stop all of that. But when I was living through it, I thought I had no power. I was afraid of being abandoned. I absolutely wanted to have a relationship. I did not have self-confidence. There are a lot of things about myself that I didn't know then that I know now... I think I will never be truly free. Because there are different kinds of prisons. There are concrete prisons and there are internal prisons. And I think I will always be in an internal prison."

Asked if she still has a relationship with her family, Karla said her relationship was excellent, "My family has never rejected me for what I did. My mother only said that she hates what I did but she loves me, and we have a very beautiful relationship."

Asked what the first thing she would like to do now that she has been freed from prison Karla replied, "I'd like to have an iced cappuccino. An iced cappuccino from Tim Hortons is what I'd like to do."

The rest of the media dogged Karla for another six months or so and then tired of it. For a

while she lived in Montreal under the name of Karla Leanne Teale, a surname she and Paul Bernardo had adopted shortly before their arrests, based on the serial killer portrayed by Kevin Bacon in the movie *Criminal Law*—Martin Thiel, one of their favorite serial killers. A camera crew ambushed Karla on the street. She walked away without saying anything. Rumours began to circulate that she might be married, that she was seen with an infant that might be her own. That she was trying to get work as a school teacher. Then Karla disappeared.

"We live well, in peace. We're handling things."

Karla had indeed married and had three children. Her husband was Thierry Bordelais, her Montreal attorney's brother. Karla's "internal prison" would be a Caribbean island paradise where the two were trying to set up an English language school. She took the name of Leanne Bordelais and the couple moved to the sunshine of French Guadeloupe where they raised their two boys and a girl. When a Quebec film crew in 2013 went to her home in Guadeloupe and caught up with her troll-like husband Thierry there, he told them, "The events took place 20 years ago. She's been out for 10 years. She's sick of it. She doesn't want to know."

Challenged by the journalist, "You say it's the past. But three children are dead," Thierry replied, "It's gone on for years. We don't care, we don't read about it. All those close to us don't read it, so we don't care. Some people will keep on for the next 50 years. They can keep it up. We live well, in peace. We're handling things."

Asked if he felt his wife had done the time she deserved for her crimes, he said, "That's the Canadian justice system's problem. They decided to make a deal, which they have to respect. The government can't do anything. The deal was done a long time ago. They can't do anything. Now she's living her life."

144

As Karla's dutiful husband sent the camera crew on their way, he told them, "The greatest, best known journalist in the world, Oprah, an American, called us for an interview. If she wouldn't talk to Oprah, we're not going to talk to reporters of no standing that we know of that I can see."[12]

"I have no interest in rebutting what other people say. I never have."

Karla had been found in 2012 by journalist Paula Todd, who described in her book *Finding Karla: How I Tracked Down an Elusive Serial Child Killer and Discovered a Mother of Three* how she 'cold called' Karla at her Caribbean home and managed to spend an hour with her. Todd noted that Karla was petite and her shiny blond tresses had gone dull and lines had developed in her forty-two year old face and her mouth had thinned, but overall she remained attractive. Todd was seated in their living room and observed Karla and her three children:

> Homolka and Bordelais's first-born has her oval face and the slight build of his father. His skin is a soft mocha and his dark hair shot with tufts of blond. In time, I will learn he is quiet, thoughtful and, after some nudging, obedient. He speaks both English and French and has a soft, gentle voice. He likes to write his name and draw pictures.
>
> Following close behind him is an entirely different creature. Homolka's middle child, about three years old, is a precocious, round-cheeked extrovert. She has the dark-chestnut colouring of her father. Her hair is a mass of shiny black

curls. She clambers up into her mother's lap, pulling at her face, her breast, her arms. She makes happy little-girl sounds.

The little ones like to move as a pack. The baby, who is barely walking, comes wobble-plop-wobbling in behind the older kids. His hair is golden brown, and his complexion baby-fair. Homolka picks him up, and he grabs enthusiastically for her breasts.

And yet it appears these three children have emerged without a trace from her body, which is as thin as when she was younger, her arms toned, and her skin polished. It is her face, though, so thin, dark and strained, that tells her tale.[13]

Todd was left with the impression that the children were accustomed to her affection and attention and were well cared for by Karla. She observed that Karla was smart and quick on her feet but had only one trick: answering a question with another question. She was sensitive to slightest hints of criticism and quick to lash back. Overall, Karla said to Todd much less than she had said to the CBC in her 2005 interview. In the end when Karla tells Todd, "I have no interest in rebutting what other people say. I never have," we already knew that.

Most recently, Karla Homolka's name came up in the case of the internet video necrophile Luka

Magnotta when in 2007 he fabricated a rumour that he was dating Karla. Then when in 2012 Magnotta was mailing around the country dismembered body parts of his victim, he used Karla's surviving sister Lori's return address on one of the packages. Lori Homolka, a cashier at Zehrs who had changed her name to Logan Valentini, was forced to testify at Magnotta's trial in 2014, sensationally revealing that Karla and her brood had returned to Canada and were now once again living in Quebec in the Montreal area.[14]

Despite the public fear that Karla will reoffend or become a homicidal muse for another serial killer, the prognosis for never hearing about her again is good, if she is left alone. Statistically, high-profile female offenders like Karla have rarely committed a new series of crimes. Whether her demon seed will pass to her innocent children, the way it was passed to Bernardo and to Gallego by their dysfunctional parents and to countless of other serial perpetrators, remains to be seen.

"Like Everest, he is there."

Explaining Karla is a difficult task. There is nothing in her history prior to meeting Bernardo that is common to that of other serial killers (or psychopaths for that matter). In prison, Karla had been administered practically every psychological test known to man and scored normal profiles. Her score on the Hare Psychopathy Checklist-Revised (PCL-R) was five; a score of at least twenty is required to designate the subject as a psychopath.[15] On the other hand, while in prison Karla completed a degree from Queen's University in psychology, including courses in deviant psychology. She could have manipulated her responses to the tests.

Homolka remains a mystery. It was not so much that Homolka was evil, as she was vacant. She was as colourless and heartless and as soul-dead as the anonymous suburban housing tracts and shopping malls she and her Exclusive Diamond Club friends inhabited. Karla was conscious of only her Beastie Boy right to party. Her family was a numb and shriveled middle-middle-class hive of greed in an age when greed was *Wall Street* celebrated: "greed is good." All her poor sister Tammy wanted for her sixteenth birthday was a Porsche—something marginally beyond the means of the middle-middle. Karla Homolka could rattle off cosmetic-counter brand names in the midst of an unfolding rape-homicide but was incapable of the simplest moral judgment—of not submitting her

sister to a rape; of releasing a frightened and battered girl when she had the power to do so. Her capacity to do the right thing was totally extinct.

For Homolka, Bernardo was as perfect as the cover of a cheap romance novel—a blond, larger than life, nicely styled Big Bad Businessman. His values were as vacant as hers and, as such, they made a perfect couple. The walls of Bernardo's study were covered with pictures of expensive sports cars and slips of paper with slogans like "Poverty is self-imposed." "Time is Money." "Money never sleeps." "Think big. Be big." "I don't meet the competition—I crush it." "Poverty sucks." *Wall Street* was his favorite movie. The horror is that there probably was not an ounce of murder in Karla Homolka's heart before she met Bernardo, and probably none remains today. Yet on contact with a Bernardo, a vapid and vacant little Barbie princess like Karla becomes an enabling homicidal bitch. We know that there are lots of Paul Bernardos out there, but one wonders: How many young men and women are out there—with moral discretion as malnourished as Homolka's—waiting to meet their mate?

Some might argue that until Bernardo met Karla he had not committed any rapes or murders; until Ian Brady met Myra Hindley; until Doug Clark met Carol Bundy. Were these women—as women sometimes tend to do when killing—using these men as their proxies for their own homicidal desires? Possibly. Would these men have gone on to

rape and kill if they had not met these women? Very likely yes.

One thing we know for sure, however; in modern history there has not been a single known case of a Karla Homolka or a Myra Hindley or a Charlene Gallego raping and killing female captives without a male accomplice. (The notable exception, perhaps, is the lesbian female team of Gwendolyn Graham and Catherine May Wood, who murdered elderly patients in a retirement home for sexual thrills.) Solo female serial killers, contrary to popular belief that they mostly kill males they are intimate with for financial gain, in statistical reality tend to marginally prefer strangers as victims, and the majority include children and other women among their victims. Both male and females kill for the same motive—control—but female offenders express that compulsion for control over their victim thorough a quick act of killing rather than through prolonged torture, rape and mutilation of their victims, be they male, female or child. It's only when a female teams up with a male psychopath that she begins to mimic his obsessions.

Although he applied it to the victims as well as accomplices of females, as Patrick Wilson concluded in his study of Home Office statistics of nearly every woman executed in Britain since 1843, "The husband or lover of a murderess invariably plays a part in causing the murder, if only because, like Everest, he is there. The same cannot be said of male crimes of violence."[16]

Acknowledgements

I want to thank my editor and proof-readers. I can't thank you enough for your ongoing support:

- Peter

Bettye McKee

Lorrie Suzanne Phillippe

Amanda Hutchins

Marlene Fabregas

Darlene Horn

Ron Steed

June Julie Dechman

Karen Emberton Spear

Katherine McCarthy

About the Author

Dr. Peter Vronsky, Ph.d. is an author, filmmaker and investigative historian. He is the author of two definitive bestselling books on the history and psychopathology of serial homicide, *Serial Killers: The Method and Madness of Monsters (2004)* and *Female Serial Killers: How and Why Women Become Monsters (2007)*. He began writing about serial killers after he randomly encountered briefly two different serial killers before they were apprehended, one in New York City in December 1979 and the other in Moscow in October 1990 without knowing at the time they were serial killers.

Vronsky is also a historian of espionage, insurgency and military history. His most recent book is *Ridgeway: The American Fenian Invasion and the Forgotten 1866 Battle that Made Canada* (Penguin Books: 2011) an investigative account of the hidden history of Canada's first modern battle and the Irish Fenian insurgency.

Peter Vronsky recently contributed the chapters "Serial Killer Zombie Apocalypse and the Dawn of the Less Dead"and "Zebra! The Hunting Humans 'Ninja' Truck Driver Serial Killer" to the annual *Serial Killers True Crime Anthologies (Vol 1 & 2)* from RJ Parker Publishing. The chapters are a sneak-preview from his forthcoming book, *Serial Killer Chronicles: A New History of Serial Murder Today* for Berkley Books at Penguin Random House, scheduled to be published in 2016.

Vronsky holds a Ph.d from the University of Toronto in the fields of the history of espionage in international relations and criminal justice history. He currently lectures in history of the Third Reich, the American Civil War, history of terrorism, espionage and international relations in the 20th century at Ryerson University in Toronto.

Peter Vronsky's website is www.petervronsky.org

Robert Pickton: The Pig Farmer Killer

by Chris Swinney

Robert Pickton, inherited a pig farm worth a million dollars and used his wealth to lure skid row hookers to his farm where he confessed to murdering 49 female victims; dismembering and feeding their body parts to his pigs which he supplied to Vancouver area restaurants.

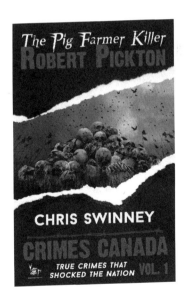

Marc Lepine: The Montreal Massacre

by RJ Parker

With extreme hatred in his heart against feminism, an act that feminists would label 'gynocide', a heavily armed Marc Lépine entered the University École Polytechnique de Montreal, and after

allowing the male students to leave, systematically murdered 14 female students.

But what motivated Lépine to carry out this heinous crime? Mass murderer, madman, cold-blooded killer, misogynist, political zealot? Or was

he simply another desperate person frustrated with his powerless status in this world?

Sources

Bernardo Investigation Review, Report of Mr. Justice Archie Campbell, Province of Ontario, June 1996

Christopher D. Clemmer, "Obstructing The Bernardo Investigation: Kenneth Murray and the Defence Counsel's Conflicting Obligations to Clients and the Court." *Osgoode Hall Review of Law and Policy*, 1.2 (2014)

Paula Todd, (2012-06-18). *Finding Karla: How I Tracked Down an Elusive Serial Child Killer and Discovered a Mother of Three*, Canadian Writers Group/The Atavist. Kindle Edition.

Janet I. Warren and Robert R. Hazelwood, "Relational Patterns Associated With Sexual Sadism: A Study of 20 Wives and Girlfriends," *Journal of Family Violence*, Vol. 17, No.1, March 2002

R vs Paul Bernardo, 1995.

Stephen Williams, *Invisible Darkness: The Horrifying Case of Paul Bernardo and Karla Homolka,* Toronto: Little, Brown Canada, 1996.

Stephen Williams, *Karla: A Pact with the Devil*, Toronto: Seal Books, 2003

Patrick Wilson, *Murderess: A Study of Women Executed in Britain Since 1843*, London: Michael Joseph, 1971

1 Stephen Williams, *Invisible Darkness: The Horrifying Case of Paul Bernardo and Karla Homolka,* Toronto: Little, Brown Canada, 1996. pp. 70-71; *Globe & Mail,* March 3, 1993. p. A6

2 http://sacramento.cbslocal.com/2013/01/31/sacramentos-sex-slave-murders-killer-discovered-living-in-area-speaks-after-years-of-silence/

3 Janet I. Warren and Robert R. Hazelwood, "Relational Patterns Associated With Sexual Sadism: A Study of 20 Wives and Girlfriends," *Journal of Family Violence*, Vol. 17, No.1, March 2002, pp. 75-89

4 *Bernardo Investigation Review*, Report of Mr. Justice Archie Campbell, Province of Ontario, June 1996, p.15

5 According to Karla Homolka's testimony of what Paul later told her.

6 *Bernardo Investigation Review*, p. 149

7 http://www.cbc.ca/player/Shows/Shows/the+fifth+estate/ID/2337732322/

8 Christopher D. Clemmer, "Obstructing The Bernardo Investigation: Kenneth Murray and the Defence Counsel's Conflicting Obligations to Clients and the Court." *Osgoode Hall Review of Law and Policy*, 1.2 (2014): 137-197.

https://www.youtube.com/watch?v=xfNpbfcJSLg

13 Paula Todd, (2012-06-18). *Finding Karla: How I Tracked Down an Elusive Serial Child Killer and Discovered a Mother of Three* (Kindle Single) (Kindle Locations 456-459). Canadian Writers Group/The Atavist. Kindle Edition.

14 http://www.theglobeandmail.com/news/national/magnotta-murder-trial-hears-from-karla-homolkas-sister/article21144303/

15 Stephen Williams, *Karla: A Pact with the Devil*, Toronto: Seal Books, 2003, p. 85.

16 Patrick Wilson, *Murderess: A Study of Women Executed in Britain Since 1843*, London: Michael Joseph, 1971, p. 94.

Printed in Great Britain
by Amazon.co.uk, Ltd.,
Marston Gate.